THE POLITICALLY HOMELESS CHRISTIAN

HOW TO CONQUER POLITICAL IDOLATRY,
REJECT POLARIZATION, AND RECOMMIT TO GOD'S
GREATEST TWO COMMANDS

AARON SCHAFER

FOUNDATION PUBLISHING HOUSE
OKEMOS.

Foundation Publishing House L.L.C.
Copyright © 2020 by Aaron Schafer

Scripture quotations, unless otherwise noted are taken from THE HOLY BIBLE, NEW INTERNATIONAL VERSION®, NIV® Copyright © 1973, 1978, 1984, 2011 by Biblica, Inc.® Used by permission. All rights reserved worldwide.

ISBN: 978-1-953676-00-9

Cover design by Ida Sveningsson

CONTENTS

PART 1: THE BIG PICTURE

CHAPTER 1 09
"GIVE US A KING TO LEAD US!"

CHAPTER 2 23
REMEMBERING WHY WE ARE HERE

CHAPTER 3 33
REMOVING THE PLANK FROM OUR EYE

CHAPTER 4 41
WHAT TYPE OF POLITICAL DISCOURSE WOULD
BRING PEOPLE TO CHRIST?

CHAPTER 5 55
DOES THE POLITICAL CONTENT I CONSUME MAKE
ME MORE LIKE JESUS?

CHAPTER 6 67
PERSON VS. PLATFORM

PART 2: THE ISSUES THAT DRIVE US

CHAPTER 7 85
TAKING CARE OF THE POOR

CHAPTER 8 99
SHOWING THE LOVE OF JESUS TO FOREIGNERS

CHAPTER 9 113
LEGISLATING SIN

CHAPTER 10 133
LEADING WITH GRACE AND LOVE

CONCLUSION 163
RENEWING OUR MINDS

ACKNOWLEDGMENTS

Thank you to my amazing wife Naomi. God truly blessed me when he brought you into my life. I could not have asked for a more perfect spouse to walk through life with. Your love, support, and grace during this journey meant the world to me. I could not have done this without you. Thank you to all of my children, Elizabeth, Emma, Sophie, and Andrew, for your encouragement while writing this book. Every day you make me want to be a better example of God's love for all of you. Thank you to my parents, Randy and Kathy Schafer, for how well you have modeled the fruits of the Spirit for Emily and I throughout our entire lives. You truly embody love, joy, peace, patience, kindness, goodness, faithfulness, gentleness, and self-control.

Finally, and most importantly, the largest thanks goes to our Father in Heaven. Thank you for taking me through the painful journey of exploring my own politics over the last 12 years.

Thank you for humbling me, breaking down the walls I had built up, and drawing me back towards you. Thank you for the constant reminder of your greatest two Commandments when I am tempted to stray away. Thank you for reminding me that none of my political beliefs are more important than loving you and loving others.

My sincere hope is that Christians, from both sides of the aisle, would read this book with an open mind and open heart for what God might want to share. Ultimately my deepest desire is that you would come away from this book with an intense longing to live out your political life in a way that honors the greatest two commandments:

"Love the Lord your God with all your
heart and with all your soul and with all your mind."
This is the first and greatest commandment.

And the second is like it:
"Love your neighbor as yourself."

Jesus

MATTHEW 22:37-39

PART 1

THE BIG PICTURE

CHAPTER 1

"GIVE US A KING TO LEAD US!"

"Love the Lord your God
with all your heart and with all your soul
and with all your mind."
This is the first and greatest commandment.
And the second is like it:
"Love your neighbor as yourself."

– Jesus

MATTHEW 22:37-39

CONQUERING POLITICAL IDOLATRY

"As a Christian, I don't really feel like I belong in either political party."

"There are aspects of each party's platform I agree with, but some that I simply cannot get on board with."

"I really dislike the way they present themselves, the divisive rhetoric, and all the hateful language; however, I agree with some policies they have enacted."

"I just feel politically homeless, as a Christian, in today's world."

Sound familiar?

Over the past fifteen years, I have lost count of how many eerily similar conversations I have had with Christian friends and family members. They all echo the same sentiment of feeling that they lack a political home in today's increasingly polarized world.

They all contain the same discomfort with the political landscape of our country, and the same sadness at the state of our nation. Between 2015 and 2020 these conversations have grown exponentially more frequent, and far more disheartening.

In this book, I will not attempt to persuade you to have a political home. I will not tell you that as a Christian you should definitively belong to the Republican Party, Democratic Party, or a third party that has yet to take hold. Actually, it is quite the opposite.

This is a book about identity.

This is a book about living out our faith in a way that causes our lives to look increasingly like the life of the man we claim to follow.

This is a book about embracing our political homelessness, breaking free of the chains political parties have attempted to shackle us with, and remembering that the ultimate goal of Christians should be the advancement of the Kingdom of God, and not the advancement of a charismatic leader, political party, or set of domestic policy positions.

This book is about remembering who we are and whose we are.

We should be politically homeless.

WHERE DO WE PLACE OUR IDENTITY?

Unfortunately, we feel the intense tug in the opposite direction. We are burdened with the natural human longing to be part of a tribe. This desire to belong manifests itself in pride for our country, our church, the high school we attended, the sports teams we root for, and in countless other ways.

All of these items, over time, become part of our identity. The more we identify with these aspects of our lives, and the more time we spend contemplating them, the deeper that identity runs.

I am a Christian and I try to live my life in such a way that honors Jesus. I ask God constantly to help me with kindness, gentleness, patience, self-control, and humility. . . except during March Madness.

Now, I am a Michigan State Spartan.

Gentleness, self-control, and humility might not be the first characteristics you would list if you watched a 'Sweet 16' game with me!

I like to think this is all in good fun. Our passionate support for different tribes we belong to can manifest in ways that can be healthy and bring us together. Although, there are some people who take their sports fandom a bit too far.

This feeling of being politically homeless comes from the desire for belonging. We would love to have a single party that represents all of our ideas, so we don't have to feel this internal turmoil. We want it to be black and white.

However, with politics, this desire for a political home can have far more dire consequences than sports fandom. If we go too far down any individual political rabbit hole, our own identity can rapidly find itself on shaky ground.

It can be easy for our identity as a Democrat, Republican, or third party advocate, to become more central to the way we think and act, than our identity as Christians.

We can begin to find ourselves doing and saying things that run counter to the message of Jesus. We may develop a tendency to defend the words and actions of one person that would have us up in arms if those same words were said by someone from the 'other side.'

We allow ourselves to become politically polarized.

Christians should be the people in our society pushing back against polarization and leading the political discourse with love and compassion. We should be the group who realizes our identity is not in a political party, but is in Christ. We should lead the charge against all forms of corruption, abuse of power, and policies that go counter to the mission Jesus gave us in caring for his flock, regardless of the party.

When we do the opposite, and begin to rationalize our way into conforming to a political party, regardless of whether their actions reflect the will of Christ in the world, our desire for belonging quickly trumps our desire for a deeper understanding of God's love for all of his people, and God's love for us.

In our desire to have a political tribe to belong to, we create an idol. When we cast aside our intellectual curiosity, refuse to adapt our opinions on policy when presented with new information, and lose our ability to view each candidate and every issue independently, we have cast our lot with a political party.

We have sworn allegiance to something or someone who is not God and was never designed to be worshipped.

Sound extreme?

Unfortunately, it is anything but extreme. In fact, it is the most normal and most consistent thing about our tribal existence, in this broken and fallen world. From the very beginning of our story as children of God, we have sought to put our faith in leaders, thus contributing to our own demise. This is first seen when the Israelites came to Samuel wanting a King, like every other nation.

But when they said,"Give us a king to lead us," this displeased
Samuel; so he prayed to the Lord. And the Lord told him: "Listen to
all that the people are saying to you; it is not you they have rejected,
but they have rejected me as their king. As they have done from the
day I brought them up out of Egypt until this day, forsaking me and
serving other gods, so they are doing to you. Now listen to them; but
warn them solemnly and let them know what the king who will reign
over them will claim as his rights."

Samuel told all the words of the Lord to the people who were asking
him for a king. He said, "This is what the king who will reign over
you will claim as his rights: He will take your sons and make them
serve with his chariots and horses, and they will run in front of his
chariots. Some he will assign to be commanders of thousands and
commanders of fifties, and others to plow his ground and reap his
harvest, and still others to make weapons of war and equipment for
his chariots. He will take your daughters to be perfumers and cooks
and bakers. He will take the best of your fields and vineyards and
olive groves and give them to his attendants. He will take a tenth of
your grain and of your vintage and give it to his officials and att-
endants. Your male and female servants and the best of your cattle
and donkeys he will take for his own use. He will take a tenth of
your flocks, and you yourselves will become his slaves. When that
day comes, you will cry out for relief from the king you have chosen,
but the Lord will not answer you in that day."

But the people refused to listen to Samuel. "No!" they said.
"We want a king over us. Then we will be like all the other nations,
with a king to lead us and to go out before us and fight our battles."

1 SAMUEL 8:6-20

God told us very early on, "Be careful what you wish for."

We have, unfortunately, always collectively responded, "Give us a king."

Why is it we have always wanted a king? Has our longing been for the king to rule wisely, ensuring that good policies are in place to advance the health and stability of our nation? Do we look to the king to form a more just society for the weak and vulnerable because it is a mission the Bible consistently implores us to pursue as followers of Jesus?

No, we see clearly this deep longing for a king in the response given by the Israelites:

"We want a king over us. Then we will be like all the other nations, with a king to lead us and to go out before us and fight our battles."

OUR DESIRE FOR A KING TO FIGHT OUR BATTLES

We want a king to fight our battles. We want a king that goes to war, on our behalf, against the other side.

American presidents have always had their highest approval ratings when first going to war. When we feel attacked, there is a natural human tendency to "rally to the flag." When we feel threatened, logic has a tendency to fly out the window. When we feel in danger, our primal instincts for the safety of our tribe kick into full swing.

Decisions made in these times of heightened stress can occasionally be full of wisdom, but frequently prove otherwise.

Unfortunately, in our world today, we have been told the enemy is the other party. Through an increasingly polarized media landscape, along with algorithms that push content upon us that the internet believes we want to see, we are shoved deeper and deeper into our own echo chambers. The more we believe one political viewpoint, the more the internet seeks to provide us with articles that confirm our existing worldview.

The Internet is extremely conscious of our primal instincts. News outlets on both sides of the aisle, Facebook, political bloggers, etc., all understand what drives ratings, clicks, and shares.

Outrage.

We are addicted to being angry. We are addicted to feeling like our beliefs, and way of life, are under attack. This is true on both sides of the aisle.

Thus, we want a king. We want a king to go out and fight our battles. However, our king is not a president, senator, or member of Congress. Our king is the party we align ourselves with, and our enemy is the other side.

We don't want a king to work across the aisle, to come up with well-thought-out policies to take on the genuine challenges the world faces. We don't want a king to listen with an open mind, consider ideas from across the political spectrum, and work with people we don't always agree with to find a mutual win.

We want a king to fight our battles. We want a king who will punch back.

Even more frightening than this is another trend we see clearly on both sides: our side winning frequently appears less important to us than the other side losing.

This may sound like an exaggeration at first. Let me ask you this; do you see more people sharing positive and uplifting content about "their side," or negative information about the other side? If you are honest with yourself, do you interact more with content centered on policy proposals you would support, because you see them as a vehicle for positive change in the world, or with content containing damning stories about the other side?

POLITICS AS A SPORT

Politics has become a sport. We follow politics the way we follow our favorite teams. We care more about our side winning and our "enemies" losing than we care about good governance.

I graduated from Michigan State University in 2004. I remember a conversation I once had with a friend where we laughed about the fact that we definitely took more pleasure from a devastating University of

Michigan loss, on a football Saturday, than a Michigan State win. Don't get me wrong, we love seeing our team win. However, for the vast majority of us, we relish seeing our opponents lose even more.

One could argue this is actually not healthy in sports either. However, the consequences are far less severe when rooting against a football team. In politics, the impact of this mindset can be absolutely devastating. We can find ourselves rooting against entire groups of people. We can find ourselves drifting farther and farther away from emulating the fruits of the spirit we are called to embody as Christians.

In politics, this visceral disdain for the other side is a poison that draws us away from Christ. It separates the children of God into "us" and "them." It unleashes the darker side of our heart in ways that few other things can, even in Christians who normally operate out of love, compassion, and kindness in most other areas of their lives. James put it best:

> "With the tongue we praise our Lord and Father, and with it we curse human beings, who have been made in God's likeness. Out of the same mouth comes praise and cursing. My brothers and sisters, this should not be. Can both fresh water and salt water flow from the same spring? My brothers and sisters, can a fig tree bear olives, or a grapevine bear figs? Neither can a salt spring produce fresh water."
>
> **JAMES 3:9-12**

If we cling too closely to a single party, to where we will follow them blindly and ignore obvious corruption, clear abuses of power, and rhetoric that is the opposite of what we stand for as Christians, we embody what James describes above. With the same mouth we praise God, we curse others. With the same tongue we profess to be a new creation, forever changed by the love of Christ, we defend indefensible actions of our elected leaders.

"My brothers and sisters, this should not be."

It is time to embrace that we were never called to feel at home in a political party. We should always feel a certain sense of not belonging because, truth be told, we don't. Political parties are an earthly creation, and this is not our ultimate home.

It is time for us to get back to desiring, not a king, but the King of Kings. It is time to stop allowing political alignment to be a basis for our identity. It is time to turn away from the sources of information that seek to drive us apart and start turning back to the word of God for wisdom.

Throughout the rest of this book, that is our goal. We will dive into what scripture has to say about how Christians are called to interact with this world, how we should view our civic responsibility in a democratic society, and how our politics should ultimately point people toward the Father, not turn them away.

Thank you for being willing to come on this journey. My prayer is that this book results in an increased desire to live out God's two greatest commandments:

One of them, an expert in the law, tested him with this question:

"Teacher, which is the greatest commandment in the Law?"
Jesus replied: "'Love the Lord your God with all your heart and with
all your soul and with all your mind.' This is the first and greatest
commandment. And the second is like it: 'Love your neighbor
as yourself.' All the Law and the Prophets hang on these two
commandments."

MATTHEW 22:35-40

Let's dive in and see what the Bible has to say about how we can best live these out!

CHAPTER 2

REMEMBERING WHY
WE ARE HERE

Then Jesus came to them and said,
"All authority in heaven and on earth has been
given to me. Therefore go and make disciples of all
nations, baptizing them in the name of the Father
and of the Son and of the Holy Spirit, and teaching
them to obey everything I have commanded you.
And surely I am with you always, to the very
end of the age."

MATTHEW 28:18-20

HONORING THE GREAT COMMISSION

There is a reason this is called the Great Commission and not the subtle suggestion. When Jesus rose from the dead his message was clear, 'go and make disciples. Teach them to obey what I have taught you.' This may sound like a question that should have an obvious answer, but if Jesus wants us to bring others to him and share what he taught, what did Jesus spend the vast majority of his time teaching while on Earth? Does the way we currently engage in politics live out the final command Jesus gave us? In his letter to the Colossians Paul writes:

> *"Let the peace of Christ rule in your hearts, since as members of one body you were called to peace. And be thankful. Let the message of Christ dwell among you richly as you teach and admonish one another with all wisdom through psalms, hymns, and songs from the Spirit, singing to God with gratitude in your hearts. And whatever you do, whether in word or deed, do it all in the name of the Lord Jesus, giving thanks to God the Father through him."*
>
> **COLOSSIANS 3:15-17**

Whatever you do, whether word or deed, do it all in the name of the Lord Jesus.

It is tempting, as a Christian, to compartmentalize our faith. It is easy to have our relationship with the Father in Heaven be something that exists while at church, during a morning devotional time, with our small group, or when serving our community in some capacity. However, "whatever you do, whether in word or deed . . . " goes far beyond that.

The fundamental questions we seek to unpack in this book are:
Do our politics, whether in word or deed, glorify God?
Does it carry out the Great Commission?
Does it love others as ourselves?

This should be the driving force behind how Christians think about their political role in our broken and fallen world. Does the way we interact with the world, politically, act to bring people to Christ? Or does it push them away?

Having a focus on loving others and bringing them into relationship with God takes exactly what Paul mentions above, the peace of Christ in our hearts and a spirit of gratitude. I have tried asking myself over the last year, "If someone who doesn't yet know Christ observed my words and deeds, as it relates to politics, would they see the love of Christ? Would they see me loving others well and want to know where this level of peace comes from amid this broken and fallen world?"

The honest answer, far too often, has been no.

I pray constantly for God to change my heart, so that I do not conform to this world and fall into the bitter partisan warfare that has characterized today's American political landscape. Our ability to reach others for the Kingdom of God is much more important than our personal preferences toward the ideal marginal tax rate for different income brackets, the best way for the government to regulate various aspects of life, and what powers should be held by the state versus federal government.

Don't get me wrong, those are all valuable and worthwhile debates to have. I love politics, which is why I wrote this book. However, these should not become part of our identity. Healthy politics should always welcome robust discussion, where we sincerely contemplate thoughts from all sides in a search for the best way to govern, regardless of who came up with the idea. However, when we allow it to descend into partisan warfare, and demand winners and losers, we lose the ability to discern the best path forward.

Now it is war.

In war, our side can do no wrong. What would be considered a war crime, if perpetrated by Iran, is fine when the United States does the same thing because, ultimately, "we are the good guys."

The same is true with politics. As Christians, it is absolutely critical that we avoid creating political idols, and then going along with whatever our party does and says. If we wish to maintain our ability to minister to a broken and fallen world, we must keep our credibility and integrity intact. We cannot fall into the trap of rationalizing away the actions of our tribe and saying, "Well, we are the good guys. I would still rather . . . "

How can we know if we have created a political idol? I believe a good start is praying the prayer in Psalm 139.

> *"Search me, God, and know my heart; test me and know my anxious thoughts. See if there is any offensive way in me, and lead me in the way everlasting."*
>
> **PSALM 139:23-24**

I am constantly asking God to search my heart for whether I have stopped seeking wisdom and have fallen into the trap of following blindly.

I know that I have created a political idol to worship when I am no longer willing to ask myself the following questions about the words or actions of a candidate I had previously supported: "If someone from the other side . . . "

" . . . put forth this policy?"

" . . . was caught in this scandal?"

" . . . had this corruption exposed?"

" . . . made that statement?"

How would I feel? What would I say about it? Would I view it differently?

You cannot serve two masters. You cannot love God and a political party.

THE DISEASE OF "WHAT ABOUT . . . ?"

Christians refusing to hold accountable elected leaders we once supported can have a catastrophic impact on our ability to reach people for the Kingdom of God. In our desperate desire to rationalize continuing to support "our tribe" against the other side at all costs, it can be very easy to fall prey to the disease of "What about . . . ?"

I think all readers know exactly what I am referring to. When confronted with the indefensible, the most common thing I hear from everyone, not just Christians, is, "Sure. That's not great, but what about . . . ?"

Pivot to something from the other party.

What about, what about, what about . . .

When Jesus walked into the temple in Matthew 21 and saw what was happening, he didn't turn to his disciples and say, "Guys, this clearly isn't great. But what about what is happening in Rome, am I right?"

He turned over tables.

As Christians, our job is not to run interference for a political party, make excuses for horrific statements made by our favorite political pundit, or deflect our political leader's responsibility for their words and actions. Our political job as Christians, when entering debates on policy, is to engage with humility and peace of mind, seek wisdom, and show the love of God to others in our words and deeds.

However, when it comes to those who would lead others astray, abuse their power, seek to manipulate Christians for their own gain, and profit on the vulnerable in our society, our job is to turn over tables.

Here is the hard part, the tables you can most effectively turn over are those with which you most closely align. It is the job of folks who lean more liberal to hold accountable liberal news networks, political personalities, and politicians. It is the job of folks who lean conservative to do the same on their side of the aisle.

Until we break free of this notion, "Well, they are better than . . . " we can never hold our leaders accountable and demand a healthy version of politics that doesn't seek to divide our nation.

When confronting the high priests and teachers of the law, Jesus did not say, "Listen, we have to consider the lesser of two evils. If I speak out too forcibly against the corrupt actions I see here, this whole Jewish way of life might crumble, and something far worse will replace it."

To be honest, that might have been a fair assessment, if looked at through a short-term lens. Perhaps the Jewish establishment losing some of their power might have resulted in an overall net loss of people obeying the various laws of God. If the goal was simply to look at the "sin scoreboard" and ask, "Will overall sinful behavior rise or fall if the current power structure begins to crumble?"

Perhaps Jesus should have kept his head down, been a great teacher, but sought only to work from within the broken system as it stood. Maybe Jesus should have gone after smaller changes out on the margins?

There is no sin scoreboard.

Jesus wasn't concerned with the next four years.

Jesus was after eternity.

Jesus was after radical heart change.

Jesus was after a revolution that tore down the religious establishment that wielded power over the Jewish people but no longer reflected the love of God for his people.

We started this chapter by asking the reader to remember why we are here. Jesus, in his last words here on Earth, had one last request:

"Therefore go and make disciples of all nations, baptizing them in the name of the Father and of the Son and of the Holy Spirit, and teaching them to obey everything I have commanded you."

All nations, not one nation. All people, not just people who agree with us politically.

The world looks to America for leadership; like it or not, the example that American Christians set is seen throughout the world. My prayer is that American Christians would collectively decide that it is time to practice politics that reflect Jesus, and his love for all human life. I long for a day where we view our mission from above as far more important than national pride, political affiliation, or any individual domestic policy we support.

Jesus gave us a great commission, not a subtle suggestion. My hope is that this book will, in some small way, help Christians reshape the way we view politics and work toward a world where we live that out.

CHAPTER 3

REMOVING THE PLANK FROM OUR EYE

Again Jesus called the crowd to him and said,
"Listen to me, everyone, and understand this.
Nothing outside a person can defile them by going
into them. Rather, it is what comes out of a person
that defiles them."

He went on: "What comes out of a person is what
defiles them. For it is from within, out of a person's
heart, that evil thoughts come—sexual immorality,
theft, murder, adultery, greed, malice, deceit,
lewdness, envy, slander, arrogance and folly.
All these evils come from inside and
defile a person."

MARK 7:14-15, 20-23

REJECTING POLARIZATION

In the Jewish world, being defiled was a big deal. Great effort went into remaining "ceremonially clean." By the time Jesus arrived on the scene, the Jewish establishment spent far more time worrying about a handful of regulations than following the will of God.

Jesus wasn't having it.

I love Jesus.

I love Jesus, not only because he was the perfect son of God, who came down willingly to lay down his life for us so that we might have an eternal relationship with his father in Heaven. I also love Jesus, the man, because he was unafraid of speaking the truth boldly and calling out hypocrisy.

Jesus only got angry a handful of times throughout the Bible, and it was almost always directed at the religious leaders of the day who led others astray by focusing on all the wrong things. They were more concerned with appearing ceremonially clean than with bringing the will of God to life in a broken and fallen world.

What would Jesus say if he arrived on the scene today and observed the way a large percentage of American Christians engage politically? If the Jewish leaders of the day were obsessed with being ceremonially unclean and seemed to miss the bigger picture, what would Jesus say we are obsessed with today? What might cloud our thought process and keep us from striving to do the will of God?

There are two separate Christian universes in America today. There is the Sunday morning church service itself, where we see amazing truth being preached. We see church leaders teaching about embodying the fruits of the Spirit, the importance of helping those in need, how we are to lean on God for our understanding, and the need to have courage to stand up for those who are marginalized and oppressed. If we walked out those doors as the body of Christ and were motivated to live out what we had just heard, it would change the world in a generation!

Then you jump on social media or turn on the TV. Here, we find a different universe entirely. Social media does a great job of highlighting what people find important enough to share with the world. Here is this beautiful platform where we can, literally, say anything we want to anyone willing to listen!

How do we each, as individuals, use this amazing opportunity?

The most common thing we see, unfortunately, is a condemnation of the other side. We are given a beautiful opportunity to bring a message of hope, love, compassion, and a positive vision for how our politics might act as a vehicle to love others as ourselves, and make changes that could truly benefit many lives.

Instead, all too often, we find it easier to get angry and stir up conflict with those we feel hold opposing viewpoints.

As mentioned toward the end of Chapter 2, sometimes it is necessary to turn over some tables. However, Jesus didn't direct this frustration at sinners, tax collectors, or Samaritans. He didn't vent about folks that didn't follow God or came from different cultures. If Jesus had one message for the religious elite of his day, it was this, "Worry about your own heart."

In Matthew 7:1-5 Jesus tells us, "Do not judge, or you too will be judged. For in the same way you judge others, you will be judged, and with the measure you use, it will be measured to you. Why do you look at the speck of sawdust in your brother's eye and pay no attention to the plank in your own eye? How can you say to your brother, 'Let me take the speck out of your eye,' when all the time there is a plank in your own eye? You hypocrite, first take the plank out of your own eye, and then you will see clearly to remove the speck from your brother's eye."

As we began the chapter, Jesus preached, "What comes out of a person is what defiles them. For it is from within, out of a person's heart, that evil thoughts come—sexual immorality, theft, murder, adultery, greed, malice, deceit, lewdness, envy, slander, arrogance and folly. All these evils come from inside and defile a person."

What would the world look like if Christians first looked internally and challenged ourselves, our families, members of our church, and our self-proclaimed Christian leaders to live out what Jesus spoke of here?

What if we sought to combat greed, deceit, lewdness, slander, and arrogance within ourselves and our elected leaders, with the same passion that we bring to debating gun control, abortion, and gay marriage?

I am not telling you which side to fall on with any of these issues. In fact, I think the view of "which side to be on" is the fundamental problem to begin with. There is a vast difference between how we feel about a topic and what governmental policies make sense on that topic. Complicated issues frequently require complex solutions. Complex solutions require leaders that seek to understand the unintended consequences of different proposals, seek to embrace nuance, and are willing to think deeply about topics, instead of sorting into our tribes and yelling at one another.

Jesus came with a message of love and forgiveness. He came with a message of loving our neighbors as ourselves and loving God with all our hearts. He came with a message of first looking inward before trying to change the minds of the world.

What would it look like if we took that message to heart?

This starts with us. We are in a vicious cycle of increased polarization as a country. We can blame the media. We can blame our elected leaders. We can blame Facebook, Twitter, and the social media age for driving us apart.

The truth is, they are simply responding to us.

If we stopped tuning into talk radio shows, consuming podcasts, clicking on articles, staying glued to television programs, and sharing posts that demonize "the other side" based purely on policy preferences, the incentive structure for creating that type of content goes away.

It would be easy to call this notion naïve. It would be simple to dismiss this concept and say to ourselves, "We are too far down this path already. Removing myself from this ecosystem will make no real impact. It isn't like the rest of the world is going to change."

Jesus wants us to first worry about removing the plank from our own eye.

God sent his son so that none might perish. We are his advocates in a broken and divided world. The world needs an army of Christians who strive to bring more people to Jesus, not push them away through hateful rhetoric. The world needs Christians who first seek transformation personally, then in their own family and church community, and then in the greater church as a whole. When people see that level of peace in our lives, the authenticity of our relationships, and our commitment to helping those in need, it is amazing how there is a tendency for people to want to find out more about that Jesus character.

Now transformation can happen. Now people can be saved.

If we first seek to remove the collective plank from our own eyes, remember how much time Jesus spent preaching on caring for the forgotten and the vulnerable, and spread a message of love and peace; the world could truly be changed.

CHAPTER 4

WHAT TYPE OF POLITICAL DISCOURSE WOULD BRING PEOPLE TO CHRIST?

Whoever corrects a mocker invites insults;

whoever rebukes the wicked incurs abuse.

Do not rebuke mockers or they will hate you; rebuke

the wise and they will love you. Instruct the wise and

they will be wiser still; teach the righteous and they

will add to their learning.

PROVERBS 9:7-9

GENUINELY SEEKING WISDOM

For most of my life I viewed this passage in Proverbs as written, through the lens of how I should deal with others that I considered to be mockers. I would read this passage and think to myself, "There is so much truth in this! There are some people who are pointless to correct. I wish they were open-minded to wisdom, but they are so closed-minded. They are the epitome of the mocker described in Proverbs!"

The fundamental flaw with this view is that it assumes I am wise and have all of the answers. By viewing this passage simply through the lens of how to deal with others, we miss the opportunity for self-reflection that we are offered as well.

This passage applies to every area in life, but I think it is safe to say that it manifests itself in today's world most prominently through politics. There are very few people who have an interest in hearing what the other side has to say, on any polarizing issue. We view most conversations as nothing more than a debate. Even the most patient of us typically only listen in an attempt to appear open-minded, as a tactic to open the mind of the other person and find holes in their argument. We hope to eventually "win them over to our side." Very little listening is done with a genuine attempt to understand the position of the other person. Rarely do we take down our walls and ask, "Is there wisdom in what the other person is saying?"

The vast majority of political issues require an incredible level of nuance and intellectual honesty, in order to discuss anything in a healthy way. Policies, at every level of government, that result in good governance, are always served well by rigorous debate. There are quite often unintended consequences of policies that are put in place, with good intentions, from both sides. Thinking through every angle of a proposed policy is something every single one of us should desire. We should all be comfortable seeking wisdom.

When we treat politics as a sporting event, with wins and losses, we pit both sides against each other and remove the incentive to seek wisdom from different perspectives.

There will inevitably arise scenarios where we do our best to listen deeply, attempt to remain open-minded, and search for wisdom in what someone is saying, and there is simply none there! The same could be said about every single one of us, on various topics, throughout different parts of our lives. However, if we go into all our conversations with this assumption about those we disagree with, we destroy our ability to potentially see things through a lens we have never considered. We become mockers. We lose the ability to gain wisdom. Unfortunately, it doesn't stop there. When we become combative and closed-minded, not only do we lose the ability to deepen our own understanding, we also limit our ability to influence others. Regardless of which side of the aisle a Christian identifies with, if we come off as self-righteous, always having the answer, and completely disregarding the view of others, it is virtually impossible for us to reach them for the Kingdom of God.

No one is going to take kindly to being called an idiot who doesn't understand how the world works. No one who is insulted based on their views ends up opening their mind and coming away wiser because of the interaction.

This was absolutely my default throughout high school, college, and in my early to mid-twenties. I knew how the world worked, the correct sides to all arguments, and felt confident in making my case in such a way that would be hard to counter.

This all changed leading up to the 2008 election. I was twenty-six at the time, and God put it on my heart to engage in an intellectual and spiritual exercise. I took eight to ten hot button topics and asked myself, "What if I am wrong on this issue? Do I actually believe this because I have considered every aspect of the topic, listened to people from both sides with an open-mind, looked at research and facts presented by each, thought through the philosophical ramifications of the position I currently support, and consulted the words Jesus spoke in the Bible?"

The next thing I asked God was even more uncomfortable.

"Is it possible that I have simply always held this belief and sought out sources of information that worked to confirm my already existing bias?"

Wow, that was challenging! For about six months I wrestled with quite a few topics. I spent time on just about every hot-button topic imaginable and really tried to be open-minded to the possibility that I was either completely wrong on my stance, or that it might be more complicated than I had previously thought. I wanted to embrace the possibility that a more nuanced approach may be necessary, more than I previously wanted to admit.

I needed to dive deep into issues and not simply dip my feet into the shallow end.

Instead of asking, "How do I feel about gun control?" I looked at the proposals out there and asked:

"How do I feel about universal background checks before purchasing a gun?"

"Should there be a ban on assault rifles? Would a special permit that required a reason to need one, along with extra training, suffice versus an outright ban?"

"Should domestic abusers and people convicted of violent crimes be unable to purchase a gun? Should they be able to purchase again after a certain wait period?"

I found that when I stopped and actually looked at individual topics within the larger issue, instead of talking about it purely philosophically through the lens of "protecting second Amendment rights" versus "protecting the public from gun violence," I was able to look at hot-button issues through a clearer lens. It became less theoretical and more practical. It became less about winning a debate, and more about good governance and the good of society.

I came away changing my stance, almost completely, on about 30 to 40 percent of topics, and having a far more nuanced view on most of the others. At this point, I am pretty confident I would get crushed if I ever ran for office, by both sides, because there are simply too many issues on both sides of the aisle that I support.

This is the fundamental problem with putting our identity in a political party as Christians. In our polarized world, we demand that every person get in line with 100 percent of the party platform or we call you ignorant. In this environment, it is far more comfortable to choose a side that seems to fit more of our beliefs, and then embrace what we are told to think by that side on all topics.

One of the biggest revelations I had in doing this exercise was the realization that politics, and our country as a whole, would be far better off if more people only agreed with 70 percent of what their party told them to support. Our country would be far better off if people looked into individual issues on their own, heard arguments from both sides, and made their own decision as to how they feel about a particular topic.

I now listen with a far more open mind to people I disagree with. I really want to understand where they are coming from. I want to know why they believe what they believe and if there is any truth in their position. Sometimes I am surprised by how well-thought-out their position truly is, even if I disagree. Sometimes, I find myself being swayed slightly, or even quite a bit toward a portion of their argument, and am thankful I took the time to ask the question and listen.

At a bare minimum, I am always thankful for a better understanding of the psychology of why people believe what they believe, instead of simply allowing them to become nothing more than a stereotype in my mind.

Virtually every person you talk to today will agree that the world is divided, and they don't like the polarized and toxic nature of our country. On this point, virtually everyone on both sides agrees! However, most of us prefer to shake our heads and say, "It is too bad the other side is full of mockers and not people willing to seek wisdom!"

I would really encourage you to consider the spiritual and intellectual exercise I described above. Don't be afraid to start from scratch.

Don't be afraid to tear down previously held positions, and then re-build them on a more firm foundation. The Bible encourages us to seek wisdom. The world already has enough mockers.

If you would like a list of starter questions on various topics to help with this exercise, one is included at the end of this book. You can also visit www.thepoliticallyhomelesschristian.com for a free print-able journal. I hope you find this exercise as challenging and life-giving as I did!

LIVING OUT THE FRUITS OF THE SPIRIT

Once there is a willingness to truly seek wisdom and an openness to removing any potential planks from our own eyes, the next thing the Bible commands us to do is to live out the fruits of the Spirit.

But the fruit of the Spirit is love, joy, peace, forbearance, kindness, goodness, faithfulness, gentleness and self-control. Against such things there is no law. Those who belong to Christ Jesus have crucified the flesh with its passions and desires. Since we live by the Spirit, let us keep in step with the Spirit. Let us not become conceited, provoking and envying each other.

GALATIANS 5:22-26

If someone was to look at the way you interact, whether in person or online, with those you disagree with politically, would they see love, joy, peace, kindness, gentleness, and self-control? Would they laugh while shaking their head and wondering, "How on earth are they so patient?"

Regardless of what your views are on different topics, whether liberal or conservative, we are called to be representatives of Christ. If we have Christ living in us, and we have surrendered our lives to him, the Bible tells us there will be fruit that is evident in our lives as a result.

For a large portion of my life, until my mid-to-late twenties, I would say my political life looked quite different. In fact, I would say that the two verses that immediately preceded Paul's description of the fruits of the Spirit in Galatians, could have characterized the way I interacted with the world when it came to politics.

If the fruits of the Spirit include love, joy, peace, kindness, gentleness, and self control, Galatians 5:20-21 tells us the fruits of the flesh include: *"hatred, discord, jealousy, fits of rage, selfish ambition, dissensions, factions, and envy."*

If I am completely honest, my younger years certainly saw more hatred, discord, and fits of rage, when it came to discussing politics, than love, joy, peace, kindness, gentleness, and self-control.

This is the problem with placing any part of our identity in a political tribe. When we feel a certain loyalty to the Republican or Democratic party, we lose the ability to rationally discuss individual issues. When someone attacks a view we hold, it no longer feels like an isolated topic worth discussing in a search for wisdom. Instead it feels like we are being personally attacked for our beliefs. When we feel personally attacked, we naturally want to go on the offensive ourselves, and the fruits of the spirit fly out the window.

Proverbs 12:18 tells us that,

"The words of the reckless pierce like swords, but the tongue of the wise brings healing."

We live in a broken and fallen world. Every year that passes, America becomes increasingly polarized. Regardless of our policy preferences, our country is in desperate need of Christians who strive to engage politically in a way that reflects the love of Christ to the outside world. The United States is in dire need of words of peace and healing from the tongues of the wise and less divisiveness from the lips of the reckless mockers Proverbs warns of.

It starts with us.

It starts with asking God to search our hearts. It starts with embracing our personal search for wisdom and desire for the fruits of the Spirit. It starts with Christians throughout the country rejecting any form of politics from our elected leaders or preferred media outlets that would seek to do the opposite.

It also starts with accepting God's grace and forgiveness for where we have previously fallen short.

When I went through the exercise described earlier in this chapter, I was frequently left saddened and frustrated with myself. I felt like I had fallen so far short of what God would desire for my life regarding politics. I was tempted to beat myself up, and then disengage from the call God had put on my heart.

If that describes you, and you feel a sense of conflict right now, that is not only all right, it is great! I still feel that way, often. I am still saddened by how easily I fall back into the desires of the flesh during heated political debates. I frequently feel like Paul, politically, when he said in Romans 7:19-20:

> *"For I do not do the good I want to do, but the evil*
> *I do not want to do—this I keep on doing. Now if I do what*
> *I do not want to do, it is no longer I who do it, but it is*
> *sin living in me that does it."*

We are not called to be perfect. We are always going to fall short at times. That is why Christ came in the first place. However, we are called to continually turn back to the Father, seek forgiveness, and turn away from our sinful ways.

If you have created a political idol in your life, now is an amazing time to confront it, and destroy the idol in the same way Gideon tore down the idol of Baal![1]

If you have become so sure of your own opinions that you refuse to hear evidence that may support the other side, and have fallen into the role of the mocker instead of someone who seeks wisdom, then now is an amazing time to repent.

If your political discourse contains more anger and hatred for the other side than love, joy, peace, kindness, gentleness, and self control, then today is an incredible day to turn your heart back over to Jesus.

As Christians, Jesus told us the two greatest commandments were to love God and love others as ourselves. Today is a great day to ask God for help living that out in our politics to the greatest extent possible.

---

[1] Judges 6

DOES THE POLITICAL CONTENT I CONSUME MAKE ME MORE LIKE JESUS?

"Above all else, guard your heart,

for everything you do flows from it."

PROVERBS 4:23

DILIGENTLY GUARDING OUR HEARTS

It is only natural that our beliefs and temperament follows the path forged by the political personalities we choose to consume repeatedly, over time. It is far easier to outsource our critical thinking than it is to dive deep into the issues and put in the effort to discern how we feel about a topic. This is the danger of tribes.

The temptation is to find a voice we resonate with, and then go full-speed down the rabbit hole. We tune in to hear the most recent thoughts of our tribal leaders on our drives, while at work, when working out, etc. When we spend any significant amount of time consuming content from a particular source, it is only natural to hear ourselves parroting their talking points. It is only natural that we begin to align our views more and more, on virtually every topic, with those of our trusted source. After all, it is not a comfortable thought that we are possibly being deceived.

This goes for any source of political news, whether conservative, liberal, or moderate. As Christians, it is so important that we take everything we hear and bring it back to the Bible. What does God's word have to say on this topic?

This also goes much deeper than simply striving to remain diligent in our objectivity, and guarding our ability to think critically about the individual topics we hear discussed. It is also essential for Christians to carefully discern whether this is a voice we should be listening to in the first place or a platform we should continue to spend time on. It is critical we begin by asking, "Does this political pundit, radio host, politician, or social media platform bring out the love of Christ in my life?"

It is critical we begin by guarding our hearts.

How can we guard our hearts as Christians? How can we make sure we are judicious in the way we select what voices we choose to seek wisdom from? How can we do our part to ensure the content we consume results in our lives looking more and more like Jesus every day, and less like the angry mob of religious elites that ultimately sent Jesus to the cross because they were so focused on their own agenda? I believe the Bible would instruct us to look closely at what these voices stir up in our hearts and where they tend to focus our minds. Jesus spent a large percentage of his time on Earth attempting to get his followers to focus less on the actions of others and more on the condition of their own hearts.

At the time of writing his letter back to the church at Philippi, Paul was going through some incredible trials in his quest to bring the message of salvation to the Gentiles. He had, through his missionary efforts, been assaulted, beaten within an inch of his life, left for dead, and was now in prison for sharing his faith. If anyone had an excuse to devote all his efforts toward instilling fury in his followers and preaching an attitude of "us versus them," it was Paul. Instead, he spent his entire letter preaching love, thankfulness, and humility:

> *Therefore if you have any encouragement from being united with Christ, if any comfort from his love, if any common sharing in the Spirit, if any tenderness and compassion, then make my joy complete by being like-minded, having the same love, being one in spirit and of one mind. Do nothing out of selfish ambition or vain conceit. Rather, in humility value others above yourselves, not looking to your own interests but each of you to the interests of the others.*
>
> **PHILIPPIANS 2:1-4**

In Philippians 4, Paul closes his letter with:

*Rejoice in the Lord always. I will say it again: Rejoice!
Let your gentleness be evident to all. The Lord is near. Do not
be anxious about anything, but in every situation, by prayer and
petition, with thanksgiving, present your requests to God. And the
peace of God, which transcends all understanding, will guard your
hearts and your minds in Christ Jesus. Finally, brothers and sisters,
whatever is true, whatever is noble, whatever is right, whatever
is pure, whatever is lovely, whatever is admirable—if anything is
excellent or praiseworthy—think about such things. Whatever you
have learned or received or heard from me, or seen in me—put it
into practice. And the God of peace will be with you.*

PHILIPPIANS 4:4-9

As Christians, it is critical we seek sources of political content that mirror the attitude of Paul. Unfortunately, the vast majority of political commentators know what drives ratings, clicks, shares, and profit. It is not gentleness, thankfulness, tenderness, and compassion.

Most voices in our current political landscape are not leaving us with a heart and mind filled with the peace of God that transcends all understanding. They are typically not coming to us with a message of thankfulness for the blessings we have in this country, preaching unity as we attempt to conquer very real challenges that we still face as a nation, and encouraging us to start by putting the needs and concerns of others above our own.

This is the reason I don't even have cable television in my house. The incentive structure, on both sides, is set up to encourage outrage. Arousing our fury toward "the other side" is a far more effective way to ensure we continue watching than a message filled with gentleness, thankfulness, tenderness, and compassion.

Unfortunately, this line of thinking can lead us down another dangerous path, when it comes to politics, which is apathy. If we are so demoralized by the state of our politics that we completely disengage, pay little attention to the challenges the world is facing, beyond seeing the occasional headline in our Facebook feed, and avoid thinking deeply about the solutions being presented on all sides of various issues, then we have forfeited our responsibility as a citizen in a democracy.

The sweet spot, for Christians, should be somewhere in the middle. We don't want to go down a rabbit hole of tribalism that convinces us the other side is fundamentally evil and must be stopped at all costs, but we also don't want to be the ostrich with our head in the sand as our world faces increasingly complex problems.

How do we find that sweet spot? How can we seek to stay informed and yet avoid voices that seek to divide and polarize?

Does this person consistently slander others?

Does this person seem to exhibit patience and prudence when engaging people from the opposite viewpoint on sensitive topics, or do they "multiply their words" and seek to drown out potential for a nuanced discussion?

After reading those questions, there is an easy way to know whether you have created a political idol in your life that might need removing. Did you read through those verses from Proverbs, along with the questions that followed, and immediately find your mind jumping to one of the following conclusions?

"Sure, (my favorite source) can be a bit biased and inflammatory at times, but they are not nearly as bad as . . . "

"Those negative things could apply to everyone in politics. At some point you have to choose the lesser of two evils."

If your default response was to become defensive of your current favorite political personality or politician, and begin to mentally attack the other side, I would humbly suggest to you that you have created a political idol.

I don't say that to condemn. I have created MANY political idols in my life and have frequently had to ask God to search my heart. The important thing is that we are willing to bring this to the feet of the

Father over and over again.

The reality is that these are tough questions to bring before the Father. When asking God to uncover any sin issues in our lives, it can frequently result in uncomfortable answers. However, uncomfortable answers should not lead to guilt and shame. Those are weapons of the enemy. He would like nothing more than to overwhelm you with feelings of your own failure to the point where you give up on this journey for God's truth.

In John 10:10, Jesus tells his followers that:

"The thief comes only to steal and kill and destroy; I have come that they may have life, and have it to the full."

The thief, Satan, wants your identity firmly rooted in your political identity. He wants you angry, bitter, frustrated, and scared. He would like nothing more than you hating other people based on where they are from, what they believe, and sin issues in their lives.

His worst nightmare is a world full of Christians living in the full power of Christ, filled with the fruits of the Spirit, and on a mission to do the good that has been laid out before them. He doesn't want you freed from political bondage.

The voice of the Father is loving, tender, and kind. If you have created a political idol in your life, God is not seething with righteous anger. He simply wants you to turn back toward him. He is ready to rejoice as the shepherd who found his lost sheep. Coming back to what the Bible tells us in Matthew 6:24,

"No one can serve two masters. Either you will hate the one and love the other, or you will be devoted to the one and despise the other."

If you did not already, please stop reading before moving on, and sincerely pray. Pray through the verses listed above and throughout this book so far. Pray through the various sources of political and news coverage you have allowed to shape your political world view over the years. Bring them before God.

The Father is faithful. We were told earlier in Philippians 4:5-7 that:

The Lord is near. Do not be anxious about anything, but in every situation, by prayer and petition, with thanksgiving, present your requests to God. And the peace of God, which transcends all understanding, will guard your hearts and your minds in Christ Jesus.

Let's take God up on his promise!

CHAPTER 6

PERSON VS PLATFORM

"Watch out for false prophets.
They come to you in sheep's clothing, but inwardly
they are ferocious wolves. By their fruit you will
recognize them. Do people pick grapes from thorn
bushes, or figs from thistles? Likewise, every good
tree bears good fruit, but a bad tree bears bad fruit.
A good tree cannot bear bad fruit, and a bad tree
cannot bear good fruit. Every tree that does not
bear good fruit is cut down and thrown into the fire.
Thus, by their fruit you will recognize them."

MATTHEW 7:15-20

LOOKING AT THE FRUIT

If we are at a point in our political lives where we are willing to take an honest look at the political commentators we follow and politicians we support, through a Biblical lens, it starts with rejecting one of the most damaging beliefs that has infected our political discourse in the past ten years:

The platform is more important than the person.

Clearly, it is important to consider all the policy positions of any person we are considering voting for. However, as Christians, there can be incredible negative repercussions when the concept of "I support the party, not the person" leads us down the path of blind party loyalty. If we allow ourselves to fall into the trap of defending indefensible actions of a candidate or elected official, or talking ourselves into policy positions that are clearly counter to the gospel message, then we risk losing something far more important than a single election cycle.

We risk losing our ability to witness to a lost world and reach people for the Kingdom of God. We risk our own integrity as followers of Jesus.

There are political figures, on both sides of the aisle, that we can easily evaluate based on their fruit and realize they are not fit to lead. There have been many politicians over the years that have come in sheep's clothing. Unfortunately, it is always emotionally more comfortable to deceive ourselves, by continually giving a pass to someone we voted for, than to admit to ourselves that we may have made a mistake in supporting them in the first place.

On both sides of the aisle, it is critical that we get back to a place where character matters. If a member of the party that we tend to vote for is found to have engaged in rampant corruption, abuse of power, or any form of activity that would lead to losing almost any other job, it is absolutely essential that Christians hold these people accountable. This starts by letting the elected officials representing our district know that we value character and want them to hold people in their own party accountable for their actions. There are few things as powerful as your phone line consistently ringing, as an elected leader, and hearing the repeated message, "I voted for you in the last election. I like a lot of what you stand for. I also want you to know that I would like to see action taken on . . . "

In many cases, our elected leaders are terrified to hold members of their own party accountable for their words or actions. They need to hear from voters who put character over "winning the news cycle." They need to hear from their voters who are still able to take off the political blinders and see right from wrong.

If the party we tend to vote for refuses to take a stand for what is right, then it is our duty to make our voices heard at the ballot box, even if that goes against our political preference. If we are unwilling to hold our politicians accountable, we only have ourselves to blame when we see rampant wrongdoing on both sides of the aisle. The truth is that a single election cycle goes quickly. The long arc of history is influenced far more by our collective willingness to demand better out of our elected leaders than our intense focus on winning a single election for our side.

Character matters.

When I was in college and in my twenties, the only thing that mattered to me was whether someone had an R or D next to their name on the ballot. The closer my relationship grew with Christ, the more I realized the problematic relationship I had developed with politics. I realized I had created a political idol and had come to believe that to be a Christian meant we must hold a certain view of government and the role it should play in our lives.

However, the more I was willing to listen to people from both sides, the more I realized there are many ways to tackle complex problems. It became evident that neither side has a monopoly on good ideas.

The more I chose to listen to understand, instead of listening to debate, the more nuanced my views became on almost every topic.

As this began to occur, another thing started happening simultaneously. I began to look more closely, with a fresh set of eyes, at what the Bible said about leadership. I began to read the Bible without my own personal agenda. I no longer read the Bible in an attempt to find verses that might defend my views on a particular topic, but rather consumed God's word to listen for the voice of the Father.

It was absolutely invigorating.

It also made me realize that we put too much faith in our political tribe to do the "right thing," while spending too little time thinking about the individual's character we were sending to represent us. I began to seek to get to know the candidates I was voting for from that point forward. I began to value what we are going to talk about throughout the rest of this chapter, more than any one specific policy we may agree or disagree on.

What should Christians look for in our elected leaders? Let's dive back into the Bible and see what God's word has to say.

WHAT TO LOOK FOR IN A POLITICIAN

PEACEMAKERS

> *"But I tell you, love your enemies and pray for those who persecute you."*
>
> **MATTHEW 5:44**

It would have been much nicer if Jesus had went with something along the lines of: "Tolerate your enemies. Try not to respond too negatively to those who persecute you. Overreacting will only make the problem worse."

Nope. Jesus said, "Love them. Pray for them." That is what Jesus commanded us to do. Surely he was just overstating this to make a point right? He was just being a bit dramatic to grab people's attention, wasn't he?

> *"But I tell you, do not resist an evil person. If anyone slaps you on the right cheek, turn to them the other cheek also. And if anyone wants to sue you and take your shirt, hand over your coat as well."*
>
> **MATTHEW 5:39-40**

I am starting to think he may actually mean it.

Jesus calls us to demonstrate radical, over-the-top, illogical, unde-served, unsolicited, unconditional love. Even when it doesn't seem to make sense. Even when it could potentially work against us. Even when folks are seeking to do us harm.

These are not a couple of verses plucked out of context to push some radical, peaceful, hippie agenda. This was literally at the core of his message.

Would folks who don't know Christ look at Christians in today's world, and who we choose to elevate politically, and see a group of people living this out?

As Christians, it is imperative that we refuse to adopt an "us versus them" doctrine, based on political preference, race, country of origin, or view of the role government should play in our lives. When we give into rage-filled tribalism, it only results in us wanting a king to fight our battles, instead of a peacemaker who seeks to do their best to govern with wisdom and grace.

This doctrine, fueled by fear and hate, is the first thing Christians must reject in a candidate if we are to be the shining light on the hill that Jesus called us to be. We cannot love God and hate his creation.

> *Earlier, Jesus also said, "You have heard that it was said to the people long ago, 'You shall not murder, and anyone who murders will be subject to judgment.' But I tell you that anyone who is angry with a brother or sister will be subject to judgment. Again, anyone who says to a brother or sister, 'Raca,' is answerable to the court. And anyone who says, 'You fool!' will be in danger of the fire of hell."*

MATTHEW 5:21-22

Jesus didn't mince words. He was not subtle. There was no part of his message that was unclear or open for interpretation. He went out of his way to put anger and hate on the same level as murder. Jesus did not say, "Love your enemies, do not resist an evil person . . . except in the situation where they think differently than you politically. Then it should be a street fight! You must win at all costs!"

Jesus said, "Love them."

Jesus knew the transformative power of unconditional love. He knew the power of meeting people exactly where they are, caring for them, and being there for them in a time of need. A heart has never been won over to Christ through hate, bigotry, condemnation, or divisiveness. A heart can only be won over with love.

As Christians, we need to prioritize peacemakers over those who would use the rhetoric of fear, hatred, and divisiveness.

HUMILITY

"The Lord mocks proud mockers, but shows favor to the humble and oppressed. The wise inherit honor, but fools get only shame."

PROVERBS 3:34-35

"Before destruction a man's heart is haughty, but humility comes before honor."

PROVERBS 18:12

"The way of fools seems right to them, but the wise listen to advice."

PROVERBS 12:15

"For lack of guidance a nation falls, but victory is won through many advisers."

PROVERBS 11:14

This is only a small sampling of the massive number of verses in the Bible that speak to the importance of humility and a willingness to seek knowledge. Over the past decade, this is one of the biggest items I began to look for in candidates when choosing how to cast my ballot. The Bible doesn't just talk about humility and a willingness to listen to wise counsel as a nice characteristic to have. It says a lack of this is what causes nations to fall.

When there is a willingness to approach policy debates with humility, we can frequently reach better solutions to the problems that face our world than if we stayed locked in our polarized corners, demonizing the other side.

We need leaders who have that high-level of sincere humility that leads to intellectual curiosity. We need leaders willing to reach across the aisle, not just because compromise is often necessary to get things done, but because there is an honest desire to look at issues from all angles. We need leaders who want to arrive at the best ideas, regardless of who gets the credit, not leaders who only care about getting the perceived win in the political media.

The Bible says a great deal about the vital importance of humility. Christian voters should prayerfully consider this when choosing a candidate to represent them.

TRACK RECORD OF INTEGRITY

"By justice a king gives a country stability,
but those who are greedy for bribes tear it down."

PROVERBS 29:4

Now the overseer is to be above reproach, faithful to his wife,
temperate, self-controlled, respectable, hospitable, able to teach, not
given to drunkenness, not violent but gentle, not quarrelsome, not a
lover of money. He must also have a good reputation with outsiders,
so that he will not fall into disgrace and into the devil's trap.

1 TIMOTHY 3:2-3, 7

The verse in 1 Timothy is in reference to leaders within the church, but it certainly does a wonderful job summarizing virtually the entire book of Proverbs, the characteristics we should all strive for, and what we should look for in leaders in any walk of life.

I absolutely love the Maya Angelou quote, "When someone shows you who they are, believe them the first time."

However, this is also a time where we need to be very careful what media we consume as Christians. There is always going to be a tendency, from media outlets on both sides, to paint opposing candidates with an extremely unfavorable brush.

As much as we can, Christians should try to step away from commentary from the opposite side, and look at the candidate themself. There are two ways a candidate can show us who they are, through their words and through their actions.

One of the easiest ways to determine the character of the politicians we are considering supporting is by listening to their own words. I encourage everyone to devote less time consuming political commentary and more time listening to the words themselves. Follow these politicians on Twitter, listen to their speeches, watch their press conferences, and go to their town halls.

In many cases, you can simply listen to the words they choose to say, with no media filter through which to view them, and quickly realize the nature of their true character. The best test of whether we are being honest with ourselves about a candidate's integrity, humility, and care for other people is to simply ask ourselves this question:

If this person was in the opposite party, how would I feel about the words they are speaking? What would the political commentators I listen to be saying about this candidate if they were on the other side?

The only way we can break free of our political idols, push back against polarization, and seek to bring the love of Christ into our politics is if we are willing to first be honest with ourselves about the fundamental character of the candidates we consider supporting.

Words are the easy part. Actions can be much tougher.

When living in a world of intense polarization, like we do, it is difficult to separate the hard facts from political grandstanding from the other side. A few bits of advice I always try to give myself when I come across a story about any politician:

1. Am I willing to read this entire article, and then do additional research into the topic if there are facts that don't line up? It is unfair for us to cast judgment based on a headline or talking point if we are not willing to do our homework. We live in a world where far too many articles are shared simply based on the headline.

2. After reading everything, is it crystal clear that anyone who is being intellectually honest with themselves would come to the same conclusion? Would we all have similar reactions to the actual facts of the case if the name was blacked out and we didn't know who the article was about?

3. Is there a reasonable explanation for this, and if there is, is this person out there giving a rational defense? Or are they simply hoping it goes away and dodging the issue?

There are politicians where it is challenging to get a glimpse into their true character from their actions alone. But just because they have no obvious scandals does not mean their reputation is above reproach.However, there are frequently scenarios where the jury is not still deliberating about the integrity of an individual. There are times where they would certainly have been fired from almost any other job, or possibly even be facing jail time for their actions, if they weren't in politics.

If we wouldn't trust them running our small business for us, working at the daycare or school that our child attends, or being in a senior leadership role in any organization we are involved with, should we trust them running the entire country?

PERSON OVER PLATFORM

In the next chapters we are going to dive into the issues in society the Bible calls us to address as followers of Jesus, and how we can begin to look through a Biblical lens at what role government should play in solving them. However, we need to start by embracing the fundamental truth that we are voting for a person, not a platform.

In an ideal world, the candidate you cast your ballot for is a beautiful combination of both. Hopefully, he or she aligns with you on more issues than his or her opponent, and also has a strong reputation for being a person of integrity. Hopefully, you agree with the majority of the candidate's agenda, and also see kindness, gentleness, wisdom, and a willingness to work with others.

THE POLITICALLY HOMELESS CHRISTIAN

However, as a Christian, the most important thing to me is that I guard my own heart and guard my ability to bring others to Jesus through the example I set in my life.

The impact that my witness can have over those next two to six years can have an eternal impact. If I lose my ability to reach those who are far from Christ by defending indefensible words and actions, simply because of my political preferences, I have lost what is most important in my life and traded it for something far less valuable.

I also know the impact it has on my own heart when I go down the rabbit hole of choosing party over truth. I know where my mind drifts when I consistently consume content that seeks to justify the words and actions of politicians that are unjustifiable, simply because of the party they are in. The fruit in my life, when on that path, looks an awful lot more like fruits of the flesh, instead of the fruits of the Spirit.

I would additionally argue that prioritizing character also leads to better governance. Even if I don't fully agree with all of their policy positions, I would trust someone who has integrity, humility, and intellectual curiosity to govern in a way that does more for the public good, than someone who clearly lacks character, puts themself first in everything they do, and is unwilling to seek wisdom.

For these reasons, *if forced to choose*, I will always vote for the person, over the platform.

As Christians we need to guard our hearts and guard our witness.

If we are willing to sacrifice either of those for politics, we have created an idol.

"No one can serve two masters.
Either you will hate the one and love the other,
or you will be devoted to the one and despise the other."

PART 2

THE ISSUES THAT DRIVE US

CHAPTER 7

TAKING CARE OF
THE POOR

Then the righteous will answer him,
'Lord, when did we see you hungry and feed you,
or thirsty and give you something to drink?
When did we see you a stranger and invite you in,
or needing clothes and clothe you? When did we
see you sick or in prison and go to visit you?'

The King will reply, 'Truly I tell you, whatever you
did for one of the least of these brothers and
sisters of mine, you did for me.'

– Jesus

MATTHEW 22:37-39

WHAT WAS THE SOCIAL PLATFORM OF JESUS?

This idea that being a Christian means you must vote one way or the other is the root of much dysfunction in many of our churches, in our relationship with other Christians, and in politics in America as a whole. Unfortunately, it is also extremely common.

I have had conversations with people I absolutely love and believe to have good hearts who have said to me, "Aaron, I just don't see how anyone who claims to be Christian could be a Democrat."

I have also had conversations with people I absolutely love and believe to have good hearts who have said to me, "Aaron, I just don't see how anyone who claims to be Christian could be a Republican."

The problem with both of these stances is the underlying truth about how we all view politics. We want the government involved in solving the problems we want them to solve, and yet we want them nowhere near the problems we don't think they are best equipped to handle.

I am going to say that again. We all want the government involved in solving the problems we want them to solve, and yet we want them nowhere near the problems we don't think they are best equipped to handle.

This is absolutely crucial for us to admit to ourselves if we are to break free from any political idols we have created in our lives. One of the greatest weapons in the arsenal of those who seek to polarize us is the attribution of nefarious motives to our opponent's every position.

THERE IS MORE THAN ONE WAY TO ATTACK A PROBLEM

Let's use the example of healthcare. When you speak to almost everyone in the country, there is overwhelming consensus on two things. Virtually everyone believes that costs are out of control in America, and almost everyone thinks we need to figure out how to bring down those costs so we can have access to affordable healthcare. We fundamentally agree on the problem. However, once we start talking about solutions, now it is time to start attributing motives to the other side. Now it is time to ramp up the rhetoric to rile up the base.

Democrats are trying to take our country all the way down the path to socialism. They hate the free market, hate capitalism, and hate every fundamental principle America was founded on. They just want to take hard-earned money out of your pocket and give it to freeloaders who have never worked a day in their lives.

Republicans are perfectly content to let you, your family, and every-one you care about die or go bankrupt because all they care about is protecting the insurance companies and prioritizing profit over pub-lic health.

Wow. That escalated quickly.

Healthcare is a critical issue. The ramifications of this can be life or death. When we refuse to accept that the other side might have valu-able ideas to contribute, we do an extreme disservice to the country. In a quest to score political points with our tribe by demonizing the other side, we put lives at risk.

The political media, on both sides of the aisle, seeks to stir up conflict with virtually every hot button issue. If we, as Christians, are still basing a portion of our identity in the political party we support, we end up outraged by topics we may never have given much in-depth thought to previously.

The vast majority of this outrage is artificial. The individual man-date, which went on to be the most controversial piece of Obamacare, was originally a Republican idea in the '90s. Back then, Democrats thought it was a terrible idea for a whole host of reasons. All of a sudden, when President Obama proposed it, as an olive branch to Republicans, what happened was interesting. Democrats all of a sud-den thought it a key piece of the legislation and Republicans changed their minds, determining it absolutely unconstitutional!

When the government gives six to eight billion dollars a year to subsidize renewable energy, it is considered socialism and complete government overreach to prop up a specific industry. When the government gives twelve to twenty billion dollars in subsidies every year to farmers, it is just part of the budget and not even discussed in the political media. One causes a massive fight where both sides are accused of destroying the country in different ways, and one isn't even worthy of a headline.

I bring up none of these issues to say one side is right or wrong on any of them. The point is simply this, there are always many ways to attempt to solve any problem. Some of them involve the government, and some do not. As Christians, just because we see an issue that breaks our hearts, doesn't mean the government is the only way to potentially impact it. Perhaps there are better ways to combat the problem through nonprofits, faith-based organizations, or free-market solutions. However, maybe the challenge actually is so large and complex that only the federal government is equipped to handle it well.

If we try to determine what we believe Jesus would have had to say about the role of the federal government versus the state government, what role the free-market economy should play versus government regulation, what the appropriate marginal tax rate is at different income brackets, etc., then we are going to be searching through the scriptures for a long time.

Confronted with this challenge, how should we begin to think about politics as followers of Jesus?

Instead of attempting to figure out which political party Jesus would align with, based on the solutions they present, I believe a much better starting place is in asking the following question: What were the main issues in society Jesus spent his time speaking about while on Earth?

We may not be able to determine what Jesus would tell us is the best solution, and what role the government should play in solving various problems, but we can at least begin by spending our mental energy on issues that Jesus cared about the most.

BREAK MY HEART FOR WHAT BREAKS YOURS

"When the Son of Man comes in his glory, and all the angels with him, he will sit on his glorious throne. All the nations will be gathered before him, and he will separate the people one from another as a shepherd separates the sheep from the goats. He will put the sheep on his right and the goats on his left.

"Then the King will say to those on his right, 'Come, you who are blessed by my Father; take your inheritance, the kingdom prepared for you since the creation of the world.

*For I was hungry and you gave me something to eat,
I was thirsty and you gave me something to drink, I was a stranger
and you invited me in, I needed clothes and you clothed me,
I was sick and you looked after me, I was in prison and you
came to visit me.'*

*"Then the righteous will answer him, 'Lord, when did we see you
hungry and feed you, or thirsty and give you something to drink?
When did we see you a stranger and invite you in, or needing
clothes and clothe you? When did we see you sick or in prison
and go to visit you?'*

*"The King will reply, 'Truly I tell you, whatever you did for one of
the least of these brothers and sisters of mine, you did for me.'*

*"Then he will say to those on his left, 'Depart from me, you who are
cursed, into the eternal fire prepared for the devil and his angels. For
I was hungry and you gave me nothing to eat, I was thirsty and you
gave me nothing to drink, I was a stranger and you did not invite
me in, I needed clothes and you did not clothe me, I was sick and in
prison and you did not look after me.'*

*"They also will answer, 'Lord, when did we see you hungry or
thirsty or a stranger or needing clothes or sick or in prison,
and did not help you?'*

"He will reply, 'Truly I tell you, whatever you did not do for one of the least of these, you did not do for me.'

"Then they will go away to eternal punishment, but the righteous to eternal life."

MATTHEW 25:31-46

If there was one issue that came up again and again in the time Jesus spent on Earth, it was the Father's desire that we take care of the poor and marginalized in our society. This was not a singular occurrence. When it came to speaking on how we interact with others in society, Jesus spent almost all of his time preaching on two core issues:

1. Helping the poor.
2. Forgiving sinners and worrying about our own hearts.

It is okay for Christians to have differing viewpoints and engage in robust conversation around the best way to help the poor. Should we focus on a certain base level of support combined with funding for job training? How could we help with things like child care before the kids are school age, so that people who want to work are able to? How can we make sure that children are able to get a great education and have access to the same resources outside of the classroom, regardless of their income level? What is the best way to tackle homelessness?

The list can go on.

I would personally love it if faith-based organizations and nonprofit organizations were able to do some of the heavy lifting on a lot of these issues, but I am also realistic and not sure the scope of these issues can be solved without some level of government involvement. It is tempting to look at each of the challenges facing the poor and individually say, "I don't want the government involved there. That should be the role of the church." If that is the case, then we better have a darn good plan on how to execute that on a wide enough scale that it meets the magnitude of the challenge. Otherwise, it is just wishful thinking and we are taking an "out of sight, out of mind" approach to the single biggest issue Jesus pointed out while on Earth.

Wishful thinking is not enough.

However, this is a challenging issue for most of us. If we feel like we have worked hard for everything we have earned in life, there is a natural tendency to feel a sense of frustration toward those we may perceive as "not willing to put in the work." This may or may not be true in different circumstances, but Jesus never gave us qualifiers when encouraging us to do good for those in need. His instructions did not come with exceptions or a long litany of the potential unintended consequences of giving to the poor. Jesus simply asked that we give.

It is easy to think, at this point, that Jesus was talking purely about charity. I wouldn't argue with you there. The challenge we face, in a country of three hundred million people, is that we are no longer a small town where there are only a handful of people in need and we all know who they are. Government has the ability in situations like these to step in and help on our behalf, in ways we are incapable of, to the level that is required.

Again, I am not advocating for any particular policy position in this book. I am not suggesting that one party has this figured out. My desire is for Christians to step outside of our political parties, and encourage our elected leaders to engage the full creativity of people from different ideological backgrounds, which would allow for collaboration from all parties. If we would stop demanding that winners and losers are declared with every large piece of legislation that is passed, choose to disengage from the political horse race, and elect politicians based on character, humility, integrity, and experience, I believe we could find much healthier solutions to society's biggest problems.

Our job as Christians, when engaging in politics, is simply to make sure we are a voice for those whom Jesus called us to serve, and to look for candidates whom we believe are best equipped to look for the best possible solutions.

One story that always sticks with me when I read it is in Matthew 19.

Just then a man came up to Jesus and asked,
"Teacher, what good thing must I do to get eternal life?"

"Why do you ask me about what is good?" Jesus replied.
"There is only One who is good. If you want to enter life,
keep the commandments."

"Which ones?" he inquired.

Jesus replied, "'You shall not murder, you shall not commit adultery,
you shall not steal, you shall not give false testimony, honor your father
and mother,' and 'love your neighbor as yourself.'"

"All these I have kept," the young man said. "What do I still lack?"
Jesus answered, "If you want to be perfect, go, sell your possessions
and give to the poor, and you will have treasure in heaven.
Then come, follow me."

When the young man heard this, he went away sad,
because he had great wealth.

MATTHEW 19:16-22

I never want to get to a place where I feel like the young man in this story. Yet, the world is constantly pulling us in that direction. In America, we like to believe that we pull ourselves up by our own bootstraps, work hard, and deserve all the success we receive. The truth is that all of this is a gift from God, and we are merely stewards of any wealth we are blessed with.

What role the government plays in assisting the poor is a worthwhile discussion and warrants a great deal of dialogue. However, I feel confident that Jesus would tell us these discussions should always be had through the lens of: "How can we do the most good for those in need? Would this government program be the best solution to solve these challenges, or at least the best we can come up with?"

Instead of asking these questions, if we spend more time contemplating how the proposed solutions would impact our own household tax burden or philosophizing on the theoretical impact it may have on the stock market and growth of our assets, we are now straying away from the will of God.

Our two most important jobs as Christians are to bring people to saving faith in Jesus, and to take care of the poor and vulnerable. Jesus painted a beautiful picture when preaching the parable of the seeds to his followers. When he got to the seed that fell amongst the thorns, I imagine it was not a popular message.

The seed falling among the thorns refers to someone who hears the word, but the worries of this life and the deceitfulness of wealth choke the word, making it unfruitful. But the seed falling on good soil refers to someone who hears the word and understands it. This is the one who produces a crop, yielding a hundred, sixty or thirty times what was sown.

MATTHEW 13:22-23

"The worries of this life and the deceitfulness of wealth choke the word, making it unfruitful."

This is such a profoundly true and deeply saddening thought. My deepest desire is to be the seed that produces a crop of one hundred times what was sown. However, whenever I start to worry about money, my career, and all the other normal worries of this life, it becomes challenging to simultaneously focus on making an impact in the lives of others. The word of God in my life definitely stops producing fruit. As Christians, we may not always agree on the best way to solve some of the issues facing those struggling financially in our society today, but it is absolutely critical that we view tackling these serious issues as one of our highest priorities. Jesus spent a great deal of his time here on Earth advocating for those in need. As his followers, we should do the same.

CHAPTER 8

SHOWING THE LOVE OF JESUS TO FOREIGNERS

For he himself is our peace, who has made the two groups one and has destroyed the barrier, the dividing wall of hostility, by setting aside in his flesh the law with its commands and regulations. His purpose was to create in himself one new humanity out of the two, thus making peace, and in one body to reconcile both of them to God through the cross, by which he put to death their hostility. He came and preached peace to you who were far away and peace to those who were near. For through him we both have access to the Father by one Spirit.

Consequently, you are no longer foreigners and strangers, but fellow citizens with God's people and also members of his household, built on the foundation of the apostles and prophets, with Christ Jesus himself as the chief cornerstone. In him the whole building is joined together and rises to become a holy temple in the Lord. And in him you too are being built together to become a dwelling in which God lives by his Spirit.

EPHESIANS 2:14-22

LEADING WITH BIBLICAL COMPASSION

There are few topics in American political life that are as polarizing as immigration. It truly is one of the most extreme cases of fabricated controversy by those seeking to maintain power through divisiveness and sowing fear in their followers. Unfortunately, it is also not a uniquely American problem.

Throughout the history of the world there have been countless leaders who have risen to power by stoking the flames of fierce nationalism, economic uncertainty, and fear of people from other cultures. This is one of the oldest political tricks in the book and has been the starting place for every horrific mass-atrocity targeting a single people group in world history. When you slowly and incrementally dehumanize a group of people with a consistent message of fear based on their country of origin, skin color, or religion, it becomes truly terrifying what a large group of people will turn a blind eye toward.

The constant questions people ask about Hitler's Germany is, "How could so many people go along with that?"

At the Nuremberg Trials, when Nazi military leaders were questioned, one of the things you heard over and over again was that they were "just following orders."

It makes you want to pull your hair out and scream!

How could you possibly get to the point where you are willing to follow orders, declare that Jews should have simply "followed the law," and end by rounding them up, throwing them in concentration camps, and ultimately murdering millions?

Hitler was not alone. Throughout history there has been genocide after genocide, mass-imprisonment after mass-imprisonment, that always began with charismatic leaders speaking to the fears of their people.

It doesn't get to that point overnight. However, it is good to remain sober-minded when we remember the logical conclusion at the end of this path. When we utilize every form of media to systematically tell a section of our society that a certain group of people is dangerous, hurting the country, and wants to destroy our way of life, we should not be surprised when some people begin to believe that message.

Our views of foreigners don't need to get to that extreme to be completely counter to God's will. The most disheartening thing for me to witness over the last ten years has been how many people claiming to follow Jesus have embraced vile messages about other human beings.

For he himself is our peace, who has made the two groups
one and has destroyed the barrier, the dividing wall of hostility, by
setting aside in his flesh the law with its commands and regulations.
His purpose was to create in himself one new humanity out of the two,
thus making peace, and in one body to reconcile both of them to God
through the cross, by which he put to death their hostility. He came and
preached peace to you who were far away and peace to those who were
near. For through him we both have access to the Father by one Spirit.

EPHESIANS 2:14-18

As Christians, the entire concept of nationalism should be completely bewildering to us. The Earth itself is not our ultimate home, and the country in which we reside certainly is not. In Ephesians, we see Paul reminding the church that Jesus coming down to Earth, taking on human flesh, and offering himself as a sacrifice for all mankind, is so that he could "destroy all barriers" and "make peace, in one body to reconcile both of them to God through the cross, by which he put to death their hostility."

If there is one political concept on which Christians around the globe should be completely united on, it is that the value of every human life is equal, regardless of the country of its origin. The Bible is not vague on this. This is not a fringe concept. It is the core message of the Gospel story.

This is also not a concept where we need to infer God's will based on the overall generic starting point of "loving others." God explicitly tells us that we are to care for foreigners.

> "'When you reap the harvest of your land, do not reap to
> the very edges of your field or gather the gleanings of your harvest.
> Leave them for the poor and for the foreigner residing among you.
> I am the Lord your God.'"
>
> **LEVITICUS 23:22**

> "'Bring all the tithes of that year's produce and store it in your towns,
> so that the Levites (who have no allotment or inheritance of their
> own) and the foreigners, the fatherless and the widows who live in your
> towns may come and eat and be satisfied, and so that the Lord your
> God may bless you in all the work of your hands.'"
>
> **DEUTERONOMY 14:28-29**

> "'When a foreigner resides among you in your land, do not
> mistreat them. The foreigner residing among you must be treated as
> your native-born. Love them as yourself, for you were foreigners in
> Egypt. I am the Lord your God.'"
>
> **LEVITICUS 19:33-34**

"'If any of your fellow Israelites become poor and are unable to support themselves among you, help them as you would a foreigner and stranger, so they can continue to live among you. Do not take interest or any profit from them, but fear your God, so that they may continue to live among you. You must not lend them money at interest or sell them food at a profit.'"

LEVITICUS 25:35-37

Over and over again, God commanded the Israelites to treat foreigners well, take care of them, provide for them, and treat them as their own. However, just like today, over and over again the people of God turned their back on his commandments.

When God eventually scattered the people of Israel across the world, listen to what God said to the prophet Zechariah:

> "'And the word of the Lord came again to Zechariah:
> "This is what the Lord Almighty said: 'Administer true justice; show mercy and compassion to one another. Do not oppress the widow or the fatherless, the foreigner or the poor. Do not plot evil against each other.'"
>
> "But they refused to pay attention; stubbornly they turned their backs and covered their ears. They made their hearts as hard as flint and would not listen to the law or to the words that the Lord Almighty had sent by his Spirit through the earlier prophets. So the Lord Almighty was very angry."
>
> "'When I called, they did not listen; so when they called, I would not listen,' says the Lord Almighty. 'I scattered them with a whirlwind among all the nations, where they were strangers. The land they left behind them was so desolate that no one traveled through it. This is how they made the pleasant land desolate.'"
>
> **ZECHARIAH 7:8-14**

They refused to show compassion and mercy. They oppressed the fatherless, the foreigner, and the poor. They made their hearts hard.

This was not just an Old Testament concept. If anything, the New Testament drives this point home even further as Jesus brought a message of breaking all bonds that formerly tied us together, and re-uniting as one body of Christ.

It also was not limited to foreigners. Repeatedly, as followers of Jesus, we are encouraged throughout the New Testament to show our love and support for any group of people society would tend to cast aside, demonize, and sow fear about. This went for foreigners and the poor; but, it also went for criminals, tax collectors, prostitutes, people with leprosy, and a whole host of other people society wanted nothing to do with in the time of Jesus.

Unfortunately, we live in a broken and fallen world, and one of the strongest emotions that results from our sinful nature is fear. For this reason, there will always be those in power, and those who seek power, who attempt to use our fear of others as a galvanizing weapon to consolidate their own power.

There will always be those people who say, "Your very way of life is under attack!"

None of us like to feel like we are losing control in our lives. None of us like to feel powerless.

When Jesus came as the Messiah, the savior of the world, he was met by this same fear from the Jewish establishment. Instead of seeing a savior, they saw a threat. They saw a threat to the very power structure within society that they had come to enjoy.

> *Therefore many of the Jews who had come to visit Mary, and had seen what Jesus did, believed in him. But some of them went to the Pharisees and told them what Jesus had done. Then the chief priests and the Pharisees called a meeting of the Sanhedrin.*
>
> *"What are we accomplishing?" they asked. "Here is this man performing many signs. If we let him go on like this, everyone will believe in him, and then the Romans will come and take away both our temple and our nation."*
>
> *Then one of them, named Caiaphas, who was high priest that year, spoke up, "You know nothing at all! You do not realize that it is better for you that one man die for the people than that the whole nation perish."*
>
> **JOHN 11:45-50**

"It is better for one man to die than a whole nation to perish." This is frequently the rallying cry, even if not said explicitly, of the oppressor who wants to maintain what power they have.

As Christians, we can disagree on the exact policies we would like to see put in place by our government to help the poor, support those who have come to America in search of a better life, and lift up other groups of people who have historically been marginalized. However, on one issue, we should stand united.

We should be united in the belief that it is our job to lead with love.

We should be united, as Christians, in our desire to seek out the best possible solutions to help as many of these people as we can.

We should be united, as Christians, in vehemently rejecting any platform or person who would seek to demonize the poor, the foreigner, and the marginalized.

On various domestic and foreign policies, we may disagree. However, as Christians, we should demand that the politician running under the banner of the party we more closely align with has a platform based in love, mercy, and compassion. If they don't, we should not cast our ballot for them. We should demand better.

When we don't demand better from a candidate who is working to earn our vote, and throw our allegiance behind a single political party, we inevitably create the worst kind of political idol. We inevitably harden our hearts just like the Israelites. Over time, their views slowly start to become our views. Their lack of compassion, love, and mercy eventually becomes our lack of compassion, love, and mercy.

As we spend time defending the words and actions of our chosen leader, we get to a place where we cannot help but embrace the truth of their message.

Then how should a Christian vote?

That is a question that can only be answered by the individual, and a question that each and every one of us need to bring before the Father in prayer. It is a question that should not be based on a single party, lest we inadvertently create a political idol who sits on the throne of our lives that God was meant to inhabit. It should be based on the words and actions of the individual candidates we are choosing to represent us.

It should also start by us remembering that the greatest commandments are these:

> *"Love the Lord your God with all your heart and with all your soul and with all your mind.' This is the first and greatest commandment. And the second is like it: 'Love your neighbor as yourself.' All the Law and the Prophets hang on these two commandments."*

We are called to love our neighbor as ourselves, and we are called to love the Lord our God with all our heart, soul, and mind.

How do we show him this love? Fortunately, Jesus gave us an answer for this as well.

> *"Then the righteous will answer him, 'Lord, when did we see you hungry and feed you, or thirsty and give you something to drink? When did we see you a stranger and invite you in, or needing clothes and clothe you? When did we see you sick or in prison and go to visit you?'*
>
> *"The King will reply, 'Truly I tell you, whatever you did for one of the least of these brothers and sisters of mine, you did for me.'"*

CHAPTER 9

LEGISLATING SIN

But Jesus bent down and started to write on the ground with his finger. When they kept on questioning him, he straightened up and said to them, "Let any one of you who is without sin be the first to throw a stone at her." Again he stooped down and wrote on the ground.

At this, those who heard began to go away one at a time, the older ones first, until only Jesus was left, with the woman still standing there. Jesus straightened up and asked her, "Woman, where are they? Has no one condemned you?"

"No one, sir," she said.

"Then neither do I condemn you," Jesus declared. "Go now and leave your life of sin."

JOHN 8:2-11

WHAT WE BELIEVE VS. HOW WE GOVERN

Sometimes it is easy to forget, when reading the Bible, that the laws the Jewish people were following when Jesus arrived on the scene were actually laws. It is easy to look back now and view the Jewish religious establishment of that time the same way we would view any denomination today in America. It is easy to think about the religious leaders in Jewish society operating in the same way leaders of the Christian church operate today, but under the ultimate rule of the Roman government in place of the government of the United States.

That was simply not the case. The Romans may have collected taxes, and exerted influence on occasion, but they let the Jewish people police themselves to a large extent. People who broke Jewish laws were frequently stoned to death. When Jesus went before the Roman governor, Pilate found no guilt in Jesus, and yet the following exchange still took place:

"What shall I do, then, with Jesus who is called the Messiah?"
Pilate asked.

They all answered, "Crucify him!"

"Why? What crime has he committed?" asked Pilate.

But they shouted all the louder, "Crucify him!"
When Pilate saw that he was getting nowhere, but that instead an
uproar was starting, he took water and washed his hands in front
of the crowd. "I am innocent of this man's blood," he said.
"It is your responsibility!"

MATTHEW 27:22-24

When we read God's laws for the Israelites, and then attempt to better understand the view Jesus had on these, it is important to keep in mind that these were not just church rules, they were actual laws. The Jewish religious leaders operated as a form of government from the moment they followed Moses out of Egypt. There was no separation of church and state. Following Jewish law was the state. When God commanded the Israelites to care for the poor, the foreigners, and the oppressed, it was not simply a suggestion to the individual person. It was a command to the society as a whole and the leaders of the Jewish society.

In the previous two chapters, we looked at the foundation of what God asked of the Israelites in the Old Testament and what Jesus asked of us in the New Testament, through the greatest of God's commandments. In this chapter we are going to explore what role Jesus would say the government should play in the area of regulating individual behavior.

In our society today, there is much debate on hot button issues such as gay marriage, legalization of marijuana, gun control, and abortion. These issues are used as weapons by the polarized media landscape to drive us further and further apart as Americans. Whenever one of these issues arises in a political conversation, along with many others, nuance frequently flies out the window. Rarely do we see open and honest discussion surrounding these topics in an effort to consider all sides of the issue. Instead, we typically retreat into our corners and engage in political warfare. We share article after article, meme after meme, that conforms to our view on the topic. We like, comment on, and share content that fits what we already believe and ignore any evidence or argument that may present another side.

This is true on both sides of the aisle.

When it comes to hot button topics, we are pretty easy to rile up.

On these topics it is natural for us to focus too much mental energy on what we believe to be right and wrong, and not nearly enough time and energy on the question of, "How should we govern?"

These are two fundamentally different questions that have unfortunately been interwoven in all our political conversations of today. Let me give you a personal example.

I have young kids and am constantly frustrated by the over-sexualization of our culture. It sincerely bothers me that I cannot turn on a television show on network television and not know if there might be a random sex scene thrown in. It is obnoxious that we could be watching a sporting event, which should certainly be kid-friendly, and not know what type of commercial is going to come on next.

If we go to the Bible and see what God's word has to say on this topic, we will find verses like this:

> *But I tell you that anyone who looks at a woman lustfully*
> *has already committed adultery with her in his heart.*
> *If your right eye causes you to stumble, gouge it out and throw it*
> *away. It is better for you to lose one part of your body than for*
> *your whole body to be thrown into hell.*
>
> **MATTHEW 5:28-29**

Adultery was punishable by death in the time of Jesus. It is clear that Jesus took lust very seriously. As Christians, should we have this as part of our platform each election year? Should we advocate for a regulatory body within the government that oversees the content of all television programming, movies, and commercials? Should this extend beyond network television to all forms of media?

It may sound like I am being sarcastic, but this is a huge issue for many parents I talk to. I would also argue that it goes beyond faith-based communities. A large number of parents I speak with, who are not Christian, hate the way women are objectified in the media and the message it sends to both our daughters and our sons.

Should we ask the government to step in?

We could ask this question about a whole host of issues. Ultimately, there are frequently going to be political issues where there is a fundamental difference between "What do we believe?" and "How should we govern?"

Instead of spending so much time asking what the Bible says on a particular political issue, it would be far better to ask the question, "What does Jesus have to say about the role government should play in policing behavior?"

Fortunately, we don't have to look far. Jesus had quite a bit to say on this topic as well.

WHAT DO I BELIEVE? VS. HOW SHOULD WE GOVERN?

At dawn he appeared again in the temple courts, where all the people gathered around him, and he sat down to teach them. The teachers of the law and the Pharisees brought in a woman caught in adultery. They made her stand before the group and said to Jesus, "Teacher, this woman was caught in the act of adultery. In the Law Moses commanded us to stone such women. Now what do you say?" They were using this question as a trap, in order to have a basis for accusing him.

But Jesus bent down and started to write on the ground with his finger. When they kept on questioning him, he straightened up and said to them, "Let any one of you who is without sin be the first to throw a stone at her." Again he stooped down and wrote on the ground.

At this, those who heard began to go away one at a time, the older ones first, until only Jesus was left, with the woman still standing there. Jesus straightened up and asked her, "Woman, where are they? Has no one condemned you?"

"No one, sir," she said.

"Then neither do I condemn you," Jesus declared. "Go now and leave your life of sin."

JOHN 8:2-11

This was not a small offense in the time of Jesus. As mentioned above, women were frequently stoned to death when caught in adultery. By the letter of the law, her penalty was death. This was black and white. There was no gray area. She made the personal choice to sin against the Law of the Prophets, and for this, she was going to lose her life.

Then Jesus came with a radical message that rocked the entire foundation of Jewish law.

"Let any one of you who is without sin be the first to throw a stone at her."

Jesus did not follow that up by saying, "Don't worry about it. Adultery is overrated. What you did was not a big deal."

He said, *"Neither do I condemn you. Go now and leave your life of sin."*

Jesus was after heart-level change. Jesus knew the Jewish people had become so caught up in legalism that they had lost their way. They were no longer focused on their relationship with their Father in Heaven and seeking his will for their lives. They were, instead, focused on personally being perceived as righteous and punishing harshly anyone found to have fallen short of the will of God.

They thought that, with enough laws, their society could achieve righteousness.

Jesus didn't mince his words when it came to the teachers of the law.

> *"'These people honor me with their lips, but their hearts are far from me. They worship me in vain; their teachings are merely human rules.'"*
>
> **MATTHEW 15:8-9**

Their teachings are merely human rules.

It is pretty clear throughout his time on Earth that Jesus had very little regard for human laws as a vehicle to enforce behavior. Over and over again Jesus brings it back to the heart. Jesus came with a message of reconciliation and relationship with the Father in Heaven. He came with a message of radical love for one another that surpassed all other commandments in their importance.

This does not mean that Jesus did not think it was important to tackle sin issues in our own personal lives. It does not mean that Jesus was advocating for the Jewish people to throw up their collective hands at trying to follow God's word and simply embrace Roman culture. It does not mean that none of those issues mattered to God any longer.

In fact, Jesus tell us in Matthew 5:17-20:

> *"Do not think that I have come to abolish the Law or the Prophets;*
> *I have not come to abolish them but to fulfill them. For truly I tell*
> *you, until heaven and earth disappear, not the smallest letter, not*
> *the least stroke of a pen, will by any means disappear from the Law*
> *until everything is accomplished. Therefore anyone who sets aside*
> *one of the least of these commands and teaches others accordingly*
> *will be called least in the kingdom of heaven, but whoever practices*
> *and teaches these commands will be called great in the kingdom of*
> *heaven. For I tell you that unless your righteousness surpasses that*
> *of the Pharisees and the teachers of the law, you will*
> *certainly not enter the kingdom of heaven."*

Jesus says quite explicitly that he did not come to abolish the Law, but fulfill it. He warned of the consequences of setting aside God's commandments and teaching others to do the same. Jesus wants us to honor God's will in our own lives and to set the right example for others.

However, Jesus did not say, "Anyone who refuses to enforce God's laws . . . "

Jesus did not say, "If you don't keep the penalty strict enough, . . . "

Jesus did not say, "The only way to keep Jewish culture pure is by punishing those who would commit sins against the will of God." How are we to interpret this?

What are we to make of the fact that Jesus "came to fulfill the Law of the Prophets," and yet simultaneously he appears to be turning the entire judicial system upside down?

How can we view the fact that Jesus says, on one hand, "not the least stroke of the pen, will by any means disappear . . . " and on the other hand, when it comes to Jewish leaders wanting to enforce God's Law, he says, "You who are without sin, cast the first stone"?

It simply means that Jesus saw the inherent flaws in trying to set up enough laws to box people into perceived righteousness. Jesus wanted us truly changed from the inside out, not from the outside in. This concept of internal transformation being more important than attempting to simply follow a set of rules, was so important to Jesus that he absolutely takes the religious leaders of the day to task in one of the few times in the Bible that we see Jesus get truly angry.

These were the religious leaders of that day. These were men who were held in the highest regard in that society. They were viewed as the absolute authority to turn to, in order to better understand the will of God and his commands for his people. They were seen by the Jewish people, day in and day out, following the Law of the Prophets down to the very last letter. Nothing was more important thanremaining ceremonially clean.

"Woe to you, teachers of the law and Pharisees, you hypocrites! You clean the outside of the cup and dish, but inside they are full of greed and self-indulgence. Blind Pharisee! First clean the inside of the cup and dish, and then the outside also will be clean.

"Woe to you, teachers of the law and Pharisees, you hypocrites! You are like whitewashed tombs, which look beautiful on the outside but on the inside are full of the bones of the dead and everything unclean. In the same way, on the outside you appear to people as righteous but on the inside you are full of hypocrisy and wickedness."

MATTHEW 23:25-28

Jesus calls them whitewashed tombs.

Jesus knew their hearts, and that they were simply performing. They were more concerned with maintaining their perceived righteousness in the eyes of society, than in monitoring the condition of their own hearts. They had lost all connection to the commandments that mattered the most, loving God and loving others. Not only did this impact their personal spiritual lives, but they were imposing this form of misguided faith onto others as well. There were two major impacts of this version of following God that had gotten way off course.

Very few people were coming to know God and embracing his will in their lives.

Those people who did convert were doing so in all the wrong ways.

"Woe to you, teachers of the law and Pharisees, you hypocrites! You shut the door of the kingdom of heaven in people's faces. You yourselves do not enter, nor will you let those enter who are trying to. Woe to you, teachers of the law and Pharisees, you hypocrites! You travel over land and sea to win a single convert, and when you have succeeded, you make them twice as much a child of hell as you are."

MATTHEW 23:13-15

When Jesus sees something that is off, he certainly does not pull any punches. I cannot even begin to imagine the atmosphere in the temple courts when this occurred. Here was a man who was teaching the word of God, performing miracles, and building a following, walking into the epicenter of Jewish culture and telling the entire group of religious leaders they were making their followers "twice as much a child of hell as you are."

There must have been gasps around the entire temple court. I am sure there was angry muttering all throughout. A huge portion of the crowd must have been left with their mouths hanging open and wondering what was about to happen next.

What happened next, was a series of events that ended with Jesus hanging from a cross.

In our Western culture we have a tendency to focus primarily on our own salvation and Jesus willingly going to the cross to die for our sins. We spend less time contemplating the fact that the catalyst for Jesus being put to death, by an angry mob of the religious elite from that day, was him speaking truth to power. Their preference was to keep the power with themselves. They wanted to be the judge, jury, and executioner.

Jesus said:

> "Do not judge, or you too will be judged. For in the same way you judge others, you will be judged, and with the measure you use, it will be measured to you.
>
> "Why do you look at the speck of sawdust in your brother's eye and pay no attention to the plank in your own eye? How can you say to your brother, 'Let me take the speck out of your eye,' when all the time there is a plank in your own eye? You hypocrite, first take the plank out of your own eye, and then you will see clearly to remove the speck from your brother's eye."
>
> **MATTHEW 7:1-5**

and

> "Let any one of you who is without sin be the first to throw a stone at her."

Jesus knew people cannot be forced to love God and follow God's Law through enough rules. We are incapable of achieving righteousness on our own. God knew this, and that is why he sent his son Jesus in the first place, to pay the debt for our sins that we would never be able to pay.

Jesus wants us to repent of our own personal sins and give our lives over to him.

Jesus wants us to bring to the world a message of God's love.

Jesus wants us to go and tell the world:

> *For God so loved the world that he gave his one and only Son, that whoever believes in him shall not perish but have eternal life.*
>
> **JOHN 3:16**

When someone has truly given their life over to Jesus, there is transformation. God, through his word and through the Holy Spirit, can handle it from there.

Over and over again, throughout his entire ministry, Jesus told the self-proclaimed followers of God to stop worrying so much about others and to tend to their own hearts. Repeatedly, he tried to refocus them on loving God and loving others.

When it comes to our politics today, how would Jesus say we are doing at that?

Would Jesus see his followers primarily focused on serving those in need, tending to his flock, and showing the type of love, compassion, and mercy that ultimately brings people to saving faith in him?

Or would Jesus see his followers more fixated on what the government should do to reign in the actions of others they disagree with?

Are a higher percentage of Christian political conversations centered around how society can best provide support to our most vulnerable and justice for the oppressed, or on various culture wars that only work to serve those who seek to divide us?

I am not telling you how to feel about any of the specific issues I listed earlier in the chapter. On some issues I personally lean more conservative and on some I lean more liberal. My point is not that Jesus would be a proponent of complete anarchy. There are some occasions where our actions are not only sinning against God but actually harming other people as well.

A person choosing to get behind the wheel of a car while heavily intoxicated is not just the wrong thing to do from a sin perspective, it can take another human life.

A company dumping dangerous chemicals into waterways clearly impacts more than just that company.

If you commit murder, assault a person, or steal another's belongings, it is obvious to most of us that there should be some form of punishment. With these types of issues, we clearly need some form of government regulation to protect the rest of society from the actions of others.

I am not saying that Jesus suggests we should never have laws to regulate behavior.

What I am saying is this:

As followers of Jesus, it would serve us better to spend our mental and emotional energy looking at how we might consider attacking root issues in our society that leads to individual criminal behavior, rather than fixating our energy on how to criminalize them.

Unfortunately, it can be easy to allow our desire to see the government enact more harsh punishments on behavior we disagree with to outweigh our desire to build a society that fights for justice for the oppressed, supports the vulnerable, and cares for the marginalized. When we prioritize punishment over mercy, we have strayed from the message Jesus shared.

Jesus was not after institutional control through more precise laws and harsher punishments. Jesus was after radical heart change and wanted to break down any walls society had put up that kept people from coming into relationship with him and the Father.

As his followers, I would argue that we should listen.

CHAPTER 10

LEADING WITH GRACE AND LOVE

If I speak in the tongues of men or of angels, but do not have love,
I am only a resounding gong or a clanging cymbal. If I have the gift
of prophecy and can fathom all mysteries and all knowledge, and if
I have a faith that can move mountains, but do not have love, I am
nothing. If I give all I possess to the poor and give over my body to
hardship that I may boast, but do not have love, I gain nothing.

Love is patient, love is kind. It does not envy, it does not boast, it is
not proud. It does not dishonor others, it is not self-seeking, it is not
easily angered, it keeps no record of wrongs. Love does not delight
in evil but rejoices with the truth. It always protects, always trusts,
always hopes, always perseveres.

Love never fails. But where there are prophecies, they will cease;
where there are tongues, they will be stilled; where there is knowledge,
it will pass away. For we know in part and we prophesy in part, but
when completeness comes, what is in part disappears. When I was
a child, I talked like a child, I thought like a child, I reasoned like a
child. When I became a man, I put the ways of childhood behind
me. For now we see only a reflection as in a mirror; then we shall
see face to face. Now I know in part; then I shall know fully, even as
I am fully known.

And now these three remain: faith, hope and love.
But the greatest of these is love.

1 CORINTHIANS 13

HOW DO WE LEGISLATE WITH LOVE?

Loving others is so hard sometimes, especially when it comes to politics. However, in his letter to the church at Corinth, Paul makes the case that love for others is the most important characteristic we can possess as followers of Jesus.

For the longest time in my life, I always thought the following line seemed a bit out of place in that famous passage:

> *"When I was a child, I talked like a child, I thought like a child,*
> *I reasoned like a child. When I became a man, I put the ways*
> *of childhood behind me."*

It seemed like an odd inclusion. The rest of this passage speaks about various gifts of the spirit including, faith, hope, love, prophecy, knowledge, and speaking in tongues. It then describes how love manifests itself in different ways. It is a truly beautiful passage, which is why it is read at so many weddings!

Then, right toward the end, we read Paul's thoughts about talking, thinking, and reasoning like a child. For a long time, I just skimmed past that part, chalking it up as good general advice. Obviously, we should speak differently, think differently, and reason differently as an adult compared to how we behaved as a child.

It wasn't until I was reading through the Bible again while writing this book that the full weight of this verse hit me like a ton of bricks. This verse wasn't misplaced at all. In fact, it has quickly become the most powerful verse of the whole chapter for me personally.

When you read the entire letter to the church at Corinth in 1 Corinthians, it is abundantly clear the church was engaged in quite a bit of squabbling. The infighting was growing more intense. The church was becoming divided. In this context, Paul tells the church, nothing is more important than your love for one another. If you are speaking, thinking, or reasoning with one another, and those words, thoughts, and actions are not rooted in love; you are being a child.

Ouch.

Politically, I have been a grown child most of my adult life. Love was not at the center of my reasoning when I discussed issues with others. It certainly was not at the center of my words and thoughts.

Over and over again Jesus brings it back to love.

"As the Father has loved me, so have I loved you.
Now remain in my love. If you keep my commands, you will
remain in my love, just as I have kept my Father's commands and
remain in his love. I have told you this so that my joy may be in you
and that your joy may be complete. My command is this: Love each
other as I have loved you. Greater love has no one than this: to lay
down one's life for one's friends. You are my friends if you do what
I command. I no longer call you servants, because a servant does
not know his master's business. Instead, I have called you friends,
for everything that I learned from my Father I have made known to
you. You did not choose me, but I chose you and appointed you so
that you might go and bear fruit—fruit that will last—and so that
whatever you ask in my name the Father will give you.
This is my command: Love each other.

JOHN 15:9-17

Love each other.

As mentioned at the close of last chapter, I am not going to tell you that I have all the answers to all the problems society faces today. I do not. I will simply tell you this: neither does either major political party. Many of these are complicated issues that require creative solutions. Frequently, the best sounding idea has incredibly negative unintended consequences that can reverberate across generations.

As Christians, we should not put our faith in a political party and then suspend our intellectual curiosity, problem-solving acumen, and heart for loving others. The debate on every issue, as Christians, should always start by asking a powerful question that stems from a straightforward command of Jesus: How can we love each other well through this policy?

Let's consider the war on drugs.

I believe that cocaine is awful, ruins lives, and has no redeemable quality. In my opinion, the same goes for all hard drugs. However, the vast majority of both parties now agree that the war on drugs did little to help with the problem of drug abuse in America and that the unintended consequences have decimated an entire generation. We have thrown way too many people behind bars, ruined countless lives, and disproportionately targeted lower-income African Americans.

At the time, it had bipartisan support.

Both parties thought the best way to combat the problem was stricter punishments. The ripple effect is still being felt today. As we still live through the aftermath of this, I come back to the question:

What would it have looked like if we had tried to tackle the challenge of rampant drug use through grace and love, instead of condemnation and punishment? What would it have looked like if we had the heart of Jesus toward drug users and drug dealers?

Would we have treated it as a mental health crisis from the beginning, as we have started to do with the explosion of meth? Would we have tried to look for the root cause of why so many young men in the inner cities thought they had no path out, and no way to make a living beyond dealing drugs? Would we have devoted more resources to parents to help with childcare while they tried to earn a living to support their families? Would we have made sure that inner city schools had the same level of funding and support as the schools in the suburbs?

> *"You did not choose me, but I chose you and appointed you so that you might go and bear fruit—fruit that will last—and so that whatever you ask in my name the Father will give you. This is my command: Love each other."*

As Christians, Jesus has commanded us to love each other, and he has commanded us to live our lives in a way that bears fruit.

The war on drugs is just one example. However, this is the lens through which Christians should view every political issue. We should always begin by looking for the root problems. We should always start by asking the questions that Jesus would have asked.

How can we lead with grace, compassion, and forgiveness? How can we love others well?

THINKING ABOUT ABORTION WITH GRACE AND LOVE

There is no other topic in American political life that has people firmly entrenched in their own corners more than abortion. There are few issues that can come up across someone's timeline on Facebook that will arouse instant passion more than the pro-life versus pro-choice debate. It is also the issue on which we seem to have the least interest in engaging with others who may view this issue differently.

Truthfully, it is an issue I am even nervous writing about. My prayer is that every reader would read this portion with an open mind and an open heart toward the other side. I am not trying to change any minds on this issue, nor do I feel like that is my place. I am simply hopeful that we, as Christians on either side of this issue, could seek first to understand each other on a deeper level, stop demonizing the other side, and begin with the question we mentioned previously:

How can we approach the tender topic of abortion with grace and love?

I personally do not believe that life begins at birth. Our youngest son was born two months early, and is now happy, healthy, and an absolute blessing to our family. He was very much alive within my wife's womb before we rushed to the hospital for an emergency cesarean section. I do not view that statement as philosophically or medically controversial. As a result, I have always considered myself pro-life.

However, I think it is important for all of us who consider ourselves pro-life to meet those who consider themselves pro-choice with love and attempt to understand their point of view before attempting to think about the issue itself.

If we are unwilling to remain calm and think deeply about this topic from every angle, we do a disservice to our ability to have open and honest discussion about this topic. We lose any chance of increasing our own wisdom in this area.

Let us begin here. I would like to live in a world where there are less abortions. I think every Christian would say they feel the same way. However, we must also remember that our ultimate mission as Christians is to win over hearts for Jesus. It is to be a living example of God's love on Earth in our words and actions. It is extremely important to begin with this ultimate goal in mind when it comes to abortion. When we forget why we are ultimately here and focus purely on how we can best control the actions of others, we risk slipping into the mindset Jesus repeatedly warned us about throughout his ministry. We begin prioritizing legalism over transformation.

I would love to see Christians united in asking this question when it comes to abortion:

Are we modeling Jesus or the Pharisees in the way we approach this topic?

THINKING ABOUT ABORTION HONESTLY AND THOROUGHLY

The trouble with abortion is that it is such a polarizing topic, we rarely have an in-depth and honest conversation about it. It is just too uncomfortable for most people.

It is time to start.

For too many years, this topic has been used to divide us. A large number of Christians will cite this issue as their most important consideration when it comes to how they vote. Is that because it is the issue Jesus brought up the most while on Earth? No. Jesus never spoke on abortion a single time.

I am not trying to say that we, as Christians, should not work to create a world where there are less abortions. I am simply saying, if we truly claim to be followers of Jesus, our priorities should reflect his priorities. The items that he spent his entire ministry advocating for should be the most important issues for us as well. Our passion for the causes Jesus spoke passionately about should exceed the topics Jesus never felt the need to address.

It is time we stop letting both parties use abortion to divide us. It is time we stop voting purely based on abortion. The only way to do this is to talk about the topic honestly.

Let's dive in and actually attempt to think about abortion through the lens of which policies could accomplish two things:

1. Help to lower the number of abortions in the United States every year.
2. Maintain our focus of showing love and compassion in our approach.

THE CURRENT FLAWED APPROACH

The vast majority of the attention paid to abortion in the United States centers around one angle, the Supreme Court. Every four years we back into our respective corners on abortion and get ready for the fight. Christians are told, "You have to vote Republican! We need a conservative majority in the court in order to overturn Roe v. Wade!"

If this is the case, I am assuming that I must have missed a headline in the last two years. At the moment this book was finalized and published, conservatives have held a 5-4 majority on the court for nearly two full years. Surely, this is the time to overturn Roe v. Wade. Republicans have been talking about this moment for decades. This has been the singular issue they have spent the most time campaigning on and the single biggest issue Christians have been told that we need a conservative Supreme Court for. The time has finally come. Pro-life people can now have our parade!

That is not what has happened. The court did not rush to take up a case that could lead to the overturning of Roe v. Wade. How can that be? We have been told for decades this was the whole point.

I am not going to assign a motive as to why this issue has not been taken up, and what reasons Republicans may have to slow play this. I do not think it would be fair without knowing the hearts and minds of the individuals involved. However, I hope that it has been a wake-up call for anyone who has ever voted Republican based purely on abortion.

The majority was achieved. Nothing changed.

I am not telling you not to vote for conservative politicians with high integrity, compassion, and the right temperament to lead, if that political ideology more closely aligns with your values. I think a healthy conservative party, a healthy liberal party, and a healthy third party (or more) is important for a functioning democracy. It is fantastic to have ideas from all sides, as long as we elect leaders willing to engage one another.

I am telling you not to vote purely based on the Supreme Court and how they handle the issue of abortion. We have now seen that movie. We know how it ends. And truthfully, it is a flawed approach to begin with.

Let's pretend for a moment that Roe v. Wade was overturned. We have a tendency to talk about this possibility as if abortion would now be illegal in the United States. That would not be the case. The result would simply be that the policy decisions now go back to the states.

What would happen then? Currently, over 60 percent of abortions in the United States are performed in states where there are laws in place specifically protecting abortion. The remaining 40 percent are performed in states where the laws vary greatly. 10-15 percent are performed in states where abortion would likely remain accessible if Roe v. Wade was overturned.[2]

The remaining 25-30 percent occur in states where there are various restrictions, primarily driven by length of pregnancy. It is reasonable to think this 25-30 percent would see a decrease, but to what degree, it is hard to predict. There would still be a large number that would happen within the timeframe where it was legal in those states, some that would probably be performed illegally outside of that window, and some that would simply occur in neighboring states.

The moral of the story is this, overturning Roe v. Wade is never going to lower the number of abortions in this country by more than 10-15 percent, and most likely would result in a decline in the single digits, if there is any drop at all.

That's it.

---

[2] https://reproductiverights.org/what-if-roe-fell

Many Evangelical Christians spend so much time on this singular issue of the Supreme Court, and in some cases they vote against many other issues they stand for. This sole issue drives a large number of votes every election cycle and, even if Roe v. Wade was overturned, the end result would barely even move the needle.

Even worse, our fixation on the Supreme Court has resulted in a large number of Christians defending horrific behaviors of politicians because they cannot imagine voting for a candidate who does not claim to be "pro-life." The end result is that we severely limit our ability to reach people for the Kingdom of God.

When we defend indefensible words and actions from our elected leaders, purely based on our obsession with the Supreme Court, we stop showing the love of Christ to our neighbors. We no longer have our focus on helping the poor, marginalized, and oppressed because we are fixated on this singular issue. We are thinking far too much about laws and punishment, and too little about compassion and mercy.

We become like the Pharisees.

WHAT SHOULD CHRISTIANS BE FIGHTING FOR

I am now going to ask a question that is probably going to make a few people angry. How badly do we, as Christians who claim to be pro-life, truly want to get to the root of the problem? How passionate are we about making as big of a difference as we possibly can in regards to building a society where there are less abortions?

Abortion breaks my heart, on so many levels. Everytime I come across a billboard, advertisement, or Facebook post with an ultrasound picture, my heart breaks all over again. I can't help but see a human life. I can't help but see my son born two months early and so many other babies that I saw throughout our month in the NICU born even earlier.

As a result, I want to do something about it. I want to sincerely ask the question, "How can we, as Christians, bring the love of Christ to the world in such a way that brings more people into relationship with the Father in Heaven while simultaneously lowering the number of abortions in this country significantly?"

On an individual level, if abortion breaks your heart, there are many proactive ways that you can help.

You can volunteer your time or donate your resources to various organizations that help expectant mothers who would like to avoid having an abortion but are not sure where to turn. There are a large number of faith-based organizations that attempt to help women who have an unexpected pregnancy in a variety of ways.[3]

---

[3] http://www.sharedjustice.org/most-recent/2018/7/2/supporting- pregnant-women-means-protecting- faith-based-service-providers

If you are passionate about adoption, you can support organizations that make this process easier and support expectant mothers throughout their pregnancies.

If you love coming alongside first-time mothers to equip them with the tools they will need to parent successfully, there are lots of opportunities to do just that.

You could choose to mentor a young woman or young man in your church family, and be a positive voice in their life. What would happen to the number of unwanted pregnancies in this country if every young woman and young man had a Christian mentor speaking into their life?

There are so many ways to have a positive impact on this issue, outside of government intervention. When we focus on supporting women through a challenging time, instead of focusing our energy on the Supreme Court, we have a powerful opportunity to lower the number of abortions in the country while simultaneously showing the love of Jesus.

This is a great place to focus our energy!

However, it is also good to ask the question, "What role could the government play?"

The bad news is that a government-driven solution is not as straightforward as we would like it to be. A meaningful impact cannot be had through a simple Supreme Court decision. This would only cause a minor drop in abortions at best while doing nothing to reach hearts and minds for the Kingdom of God.

The good news is that far more effective government-driven solutions can be found exactly where we would hope they could. They can be found by coming back to the core message Jesus advanced while on Earth, and where we started this section of the book.

They can be found by striving to eradicate poverty.

The pro-life movement has historically had a tendency to focus too much of our energy on the macro level through attempting to restrict access to abortions. A far more effective approach would be to put our time and resources into supporting the lives of the individual women, and advocating for public policies that combat the systemic drivers of abortion in our country.

When looking at the statistics, 12.9 percent of women in the United States live below the poverty line [4] (under $12,490 of annual income for an individual in 2020), and yet they account for 50 percent of the abortions in the United States. When you include women above the poverty line, but classified as low income (making between $13,000-$25,000 a year) the statistics jump to 75 percent.[5] These numbers are staggering.

---

[4] https://www.usatoday.com/story/money/2019/11/06/united-states-poverty-rate-for-every-group/40546247/

[5] https://www.guttmacher.org/fact-sheet/unintended-pregnancy-united-states#

If we, as pro-life Christians, are serious about truly moving the needle on abortion, we need to stop focusing on the Supreme Court and start focusing on poverty.

This should be exciting news for Christians!

Focusing on the root issues in our society that drive a high percentage of abortions will not only help reduce the number of abortions in the United States far more than overturning Roe vs. Wade ever could, but is also directly in line with our other, and far more important goal as Christians.

It is in line with showing the love of Jesus to a broken world, so we can bring more people to saving faith in Jesus.

FIGHTING POVERTY

This is not a book designed to deep dive into specific policy positions that could potentially combat poverty in this country. We are not going to take a microscope to universal basic income, raising the minimum wage, healthcare, right-to-work laws, universal preschool, or a whole host of other ideas that could potentially work to fight poverty. If you would like to learn more about some of the proposals out there I would strongly encourage you to look at the actual websites of your elected leaders and people running for office from both sides of the aisle. Spend real time digesting their proposals. Do some additional research on the proposals that intrigue you. There is real power in doing our own homework on these issues and wrestling with the best ways to approach them.

I am not here to tell you which ideas you should or should not support.

That is not the purpose of this book. As we have stated from the beginning, this is not a book advocating for a specific party or a specific set of policies. It is a book meant to encourage readers to break free of this mindset to begin with. My hope is that you come away from this book with a solid Biblical foundation to build your political life around, which starts by asking two primary questions:

How did Jesus encourage his followers to engage with the world?

When thinking about having an impact on society, what was the foundation of the message Jesus shared while on Earth?

Whatever specific policies you eventually land on in your own political exploration, there can be no doubt that helping those in need was absolutely foundational to the message of Jesus. A deep desire to conquer that challenge is where we should start the conversation.

Whenever I read any book, I am fascinated with how the author chooses to conclude their writings. This is most interesting to me when it is a biography. When a writer pens a biography, where they choose to end the story tells us quite a bit about the message they want a reader to come away with.

With that in mind, how did the different authors of the four gospels choose to bring to a close their telling of the life of Jesus? When God inspired Matthew, Mark, Luke, and John to put on paper the life and mission of his son, what was the final message we were left with?

In Luke, we read about the disciples returning to worship God after Jesus ascended into Heaven. In Matthew and Mark we see the same story ending in the Great Commission, with Jesus sending his disciples to all of the nations to spread the good news, and no longer strictly focusing on their own nation of Israel.

A focus on worship.

A focus on reaching out beyond our own race, culture, and nationality to reach hearts and minds for Jesus.

What do we see in John?

FEED MY SHEEP

Afterward Jesus appeared again to his disciples, by the Sea of Galilee. It happened this way: Simon Peter, Thomas (also known as Didymus), Nathanael from Cana in Galilee, the sons of Zebedee, and two other disciples were together. "I'm going out to fish," Simon Peter told them, and they said, "We'll go with you." So they went out and got into the boat, but that night they caught nothing.

Early in the morning, Jesus stood on the shore, but the disciples did not realize that it was Jesus.

He called out to them,
"Friends, haven't you any fish?"

"No," they answered.

He said, "Throw your net on the right side of the boat and
you will find some." When they did, they were unable to haul the
net in because of the large number of fish.

Then the disciple whom Jesus loved said to Peter, "It is the Lord!"
As soon as Simon Peter heard him say, "It is the Lord," he wrapped
his outer garment around him (for he had taken it off) and jumped
into the water. The other disciples followed in the boat, towing the
net full of fish, for they were not far from shore, about a hundred
yards. When they landed, they saw a fire of burning coals
there with fish on it, and some bread.

Jesus said to them, "Bring some of the fish you have just caught."
So Simon Peter climbed back into the boat and dragged the net
ashore. It was full of large fish, 153, but even with so many the net
was not torn. Jesus said to them, "Come and have breakfast." None
of the disciples dared ask him, "Who are you?" They knew it was the
Lord. Jesus came, took the bread and gave it to them, and did the
same with the fish. This was now the third time Jesus appeared to
his disciples after he was raised from the dead.

When they had finished eating, Jesus said to Simon Peter,
"Simon son of John, do you love me more than these?"

"Yes, Lord," he said, "you know that I love you."

Jesus said, "Feed my lambs."

Again Jesus said, "Simon son of John, do you love me?"

He answered, "Yes, Lord, you know that I love you."

Jesus said, "Take care of my sheep."

The third time he said to him, "Simon son of John, do you love me?"

Peter was hurt because Jesus asked him the third time,
"Do you love me?" He said, "Lord, you know all things; you know
that I love you." Jesus said, "Feed my sheep."

JOHN 21:1-17

This passage has been absolutely wrecking me. When writing this portion of the book, I wept.

I picture myself in Peter's shoes. I think about Jesus asking, "Aaron, do you love me?"

"Of course I do."

"Feed my sheep."

Three times. Repeating the same question over and over again.

Does Jesus doubt my love for him? Is he just trying to drive home a point?

Then I consider my own stubborn heart. I consider how much my view of the poor, oppressed, and marginalized has been shaped by our culture, and how little of my view has been shaped by Jesus.

And I weep.

For almost my entire life, when the topic of how to address poverty in this country would come up, my knee-jerk reaction was to respond with:

"Sure. Absolutely. We need some type of safety net . . . *BUT* we need to make sure we don't go too far and take away their incentive to work."

I focused very little energy on the first half of that sentence and all sorts of mental energy on everything after the "but." I spent very little time engaging in creative problem-solving, thinking deeply about the issues, and contemplating how we could get to the root issues that caused poverty in the first place. I was almost always focused on not being too generous.

"Aaron, do you love me?"

"Lord, you know I do. I read the Bible. I go to church. I listen to worship music. I am in a small group."

"Feed my sheep."

"But Lord, how do I know they won't use that money to buy drugs? A lot of those people will sit at home, watch TV, and live off the charity of people doing all the work."

"Aaron, do you love me?"

"Lord, you know I do."

"Take care of my lambs."

"But Lord, won't free-market capitalism naturally give people the opportunity to take care of themselves if they are willing to work for it?"

"Aaron, do you love me?"

I had been so conditioned by our society that my natural instinct was to think of all the possible downsides of too much generosity toward the poor in our society.

My first thoughts almost never went to the single mom with three kids, working two jobs, barely able to see her children, and still not able to pay her bills consistently.

My first thoughts almost never went to empathy for the homeless person standing on the corner, wondering what occurred throughout their life to bring them to this point, and how I might be able to help.

My first thoughts almost never went to the family of four barely making above minimum wage and unable to afford healthcare.

My first thoughts were almost always, "How can we make sure we aren't too generous, so that we avoid unintended consequences? How do we make sure we incentivize work properly?"

"Peter was hurt because Jesus asked him the third time, 'Do you love me?'"

This section of John has brought me to my knees because I have begun relating so profoundly with Peter. Why does Jesus doubt my love so much that he has to ask over and over and over again? Why does he feel the need to emphasize repeatedly that we, as his followers, are to feed his sheep?

The reason is simple. Jesus knows the world is going to do everything it can to make sure I miss the message.

I am not saying we shouldn't attempt to strike a healthy balance with social programs in our country. That is an extremely worthwhile conversation. However, as Christians, our natural tendency should always be to fall too far on the side of supporting the poor, oppressed, and marginalized, and not the other way around. If we are accidentally too far in one direction, Christians should be unified in our desire to accidentally err on the side of generosity, love, and compassion.

Too often in my life I have allowed political philosophy, intellectual sparring, and the thirst for debate cloud my ability to see beyond the topic being discussed, to the actual lives it would impact.

I was focused on policy instead of people.

"Going on from that place, he went into their synagogue, and a man with a shriveled hand was there. Looking for a reason to bring charges against Jesus, they asked him, 'Is it lawful to heal on the Sabbath?' He said to them, 'If any of you has a sheep and it falls into a pit on the Sabbath, will you not take hold of it and lift it out? How much more valuable is a person than a sheep! Therefore it is lawful to do good on the Sabbath.'

Then he said to the man, 'Stretch out your hand.' So he stretched it out and it was completely restored, just as sound as the other. But the Pharisees went out and plotted how they might kill Jesus."

MATTHEW 12:9-14

This has always been the tendency of human beings. Jesus confronts this mindset over and over again throughout his ministry.

I love this story. There have been many times in my life where I have been confronted with this same heart-level issue that Jesus had to deal with when talking to the Pharisees.

Philosophizing about a specific policy versus looking at the actual person in need.

There are some situations where this is extremely difficult. The answer is not clear on potential unintended consequences. However, when difficulties arise, we would all benefit from taking the approach that Jesus took. We simply need to ask the question:

"How much more valuable is a person than whatever nuanced semantics we are debating at that time?"

The direction we should head becomes incredibly clear, a large percentage of the time, when we take ourselves out of the equation, remove our own biases and agenda, avoid thinking about how this decision impacts ourselves, and focus on loving others by asking, "How can I do right by them?"

This is not just about taking care of people's physical needs, it is about showing the love of God to his people on Earth.

> *What good is it, my brothers and sisters, if someone claims*
> *to have faith but has no deeds? Can such faith save them? Suppo-*
> *se a brother or a sister is without clothes and daily food. If one of*
> *you says to them, "Go in peace; keep warm and well fed," but does*
> *nothing about their physical needs, what good is it? In the same way,*
> *faith by itself, if it is not accompanied by action, is dead.*
>
> **JAMES 2:14-17**

People who do not yet know Jesus are not impressed with our legalism. They are not wowed with our ability to prove to them that we are on the correct side of a debate. They are not won over, and overcome by a sudden desire to learn more about the love of Jesus, because of our ability to clearly show why not helping others is "the right thing to do," based on a fear that we may help too much.

Hearts are won over by the love Jesus shows.

Time and time again, throughout his preaching, Jesus showed us that he is a "spirit of the law" guy. This applied to the actual laws of the day when he was around, as well as to the motives in our hearts. Jesus told us repeatedly that our Father in Heaven is fully capable of dealing with the sin in the lives of others. Our job is to worry about the plank in our own eye, and focus on the greatest of God's commandments.

Jesus wants us to demonstrate for the world the radical, over-the-top, undeserved love that the Father in Heaven has shown us. He wants us to always begin by asking, "How much more valuable is a person?"

On this rock I will build my politics. I hope you will join me.

RENEWING OUR MINDS

Therefore, I urge you, brothers and sisters,
in view of God's mercy, to offer your bodies as a
living sacrifice, holy and pleasing to God—this is
your true and proper worship. Do not conform to
the pattern of this world, but be transformed by the
renewing of your mind. Then you will be able to test
and approve what God's will is—his good,
pleasing and perfect will.

ROMANS 12:1-2

NO LONGER CONFORMING
TO THE PATTERN OF THIS WORLD

If Christians are to engage in politics in a way that keeps the love of Jesus at the center of it all, it is going to take a renewing of our minds.

There are many people we have the opportunity to minister to in our normal day-to-day lives if we are willing to embrace God's good, pleasing, and perfect will. When we offer ourselves up as a living sacrifice, very quickly we see these opportunities pop up where we work, when online, at our church, and everywhere we go.

One of the reasons that I love Romans 12 is that Paul goes on to tackle the "how" in beautiful brevity. Paul is not long-winded in his advice on what a transformed mind looks like. This entire passage is worth reading over and over again throughout the coming weeks to truly internalize it.

Unfortunately, conforming to this world is a desire that is always there and powerful indeed! This is the age old question: How do we stay 'in the world' so that we can have a maximum impact, without becoming 'of the world' and conforming to what society tells us we are supposed to chase after?

Let's look at Paul's advice to the Romans:

Love must be sincere. Hate what is evil; cling to what is good. Be devoted to one another in love. Honor one another above yourselves. Never be lacking in zeal, but keep your spiritual fervor, serving the Lord. Be joyful in hope, patient in affliction, faithful in prayer. Share with the Lord's people who are in need. Practice hospitality.

Bless those who persecute you; bless and do not curse. Rejoice with those who rejoice; mourn with those who mourn. Live in harmony with one another. Do not be proud, but be willing to associate with people of low position. Do not be conceited.

Do not repay anyone evil for evil. Be careful to do what is right in the eyes of everyone. If it is possible, as far as it depends on you, live at peace with everyone. Do not take revenge, my dear friends, but leave room for God's wrath, for it is written: "It is mine to avenge; I will repay," says the Lord. On the contrary:

"If your enemy is hungry, feed him; if he is thirsty, give him something to drink. In doing this, you will heap burning coals on his head." Do not be overcome by evil, but overcome evil with good.

ROMANS 12:9-21

My hope is that this book gave you some tangible way to do this. My prayer is that you come away refocused on accepting the love of the Father in your own life.

The idols are everywhere and they long to be worshipped. Being transformed by the renewing of our mind sounds fantastic, but how do we do it?

Our hearts and minds are transformed by love. They are transformed by focusing entirely on loving others, serving others, supporting others, and rejoicing with others. Conforming to this world pushes us in the opposite direction.

That passage contains many simple and direct calls to action.

If you want to see true transformation in your life and a renewing of your political mind, it is going to take a lot of intentional effort.

Here is my thirty-day challenge for you:

1. A FAST FROM DIVISIVENESS

Take a thirty-day fast from any political coverage, podcasts, radio shows, television programs, or websites that use divisive rhetoric. Turn them off. All of them. In this area, we are going to need to be honest with ourselves and willing to bring this before God in prayer. We tend to be extremely good at picking out divisive rhetoric when it is coming from the "other side" and tend to have a MASSIVE plank in our own eyes when it comes to divisive rhetoric that we tend to agree with.

2. HONESTLY LOOK AT CANDIDATES AND LEADERS

I think it is important to stay informed, so I encourage you to visit the websites of various candidates and elected officials. Read their actual policy proposals. See what issues they choose to highlight. Instead of scrolling Twitter and getting angry based on the words of pundits, just go on Twitter, visit the actual candidate or elected leader's own page, and see what words they put out into the world. Let these people speak to you in their own voice, without the filter of the media on either side of the aisle. Look at their character and priorities and decide whether they are fit to lead.

3. FOCUS ON GOD'S WORD

Save Romans 12 on your phone where you can access it with a single click from an app or website. If you are not sure how to do this ask a technologically savvy friend. Every time you grab your phone purely out of habit, to go to Facebook, Twitter, YouTube, a podcast, app, etc., go and read Romans 12. Make a decision to replace your normal habit of consuming content the world pushes on us with a simple, one-minute, beautiful reminder of what we are called to live out as followers of Jesus.

If you form this habit of constantly reminding yourself, all day long, to live a life focused on loving God and loving others, instead of worshipping the false idols our society places in front of us, you will see a renewing of your mind and the type of transformation that God has promised us. This is not going to be easy. Every idol we set up in our life has to be torn down again and again and again.

Jesus constantly waits for us to turn back to him so that he can ask the simple question, "Aaron, do you love me?"

I no longer want to feel hurt, as Peter did, when asked this question. I want my mind renewed and life transformed, the way God has promised.

God is always faithful.

There is a lot of work to be done in our polarized world. This shift away from political parties as idols and back toward the good, pleasing, and perfect will of God is going to take a lot of time and effort.

Be encouraged.

> *"Let us not become weary in doing good,*
> *for at the proper time we will reap a harvest*
> *if we do not give up."*
>
> **GALATIANS 6:9**

Let's not give up. Let's not grow weary in doing good. God's will for our lives is worth the effort.

> *"Then he said to his disciples, 'The harvest is plentiful but the workers are few. Ask the Lord of the harvest, therefore, to send out workers into his harvest field.'"*
>
> **MATTHEW 9:37-38**

Let's get out into the fields and get to work!

ROMANS 12

POLITICAL JOURNAL

Do not conform to the pattern of this world,
but be transformed by the renewing of your mind. Then
you will be able to test and approve what God's will is—
his good, pleasing and perfect will.

ROMANS 12:2

RENEWING OUR MINDS

If we are serious about renewing our minds, when it comes to our approach to politics, it is going to take work. We are constantly surrounded by messages that push us in the direction of polarization. Conforming to the pattern of this world is natural. Renewing our minds requires time in prayer, scripture, and contemplation.

In this journal, there is space for you to do exactly that.

Throughout different sections of "The Politically Homeless Christian", there were questions posed for the reader to think and pray about. This journal gives you a place to come to the Father and wrestle with some of these tough questions.
This is broken up into two parts.

1. 30 days of renewing our mind through scripture
2. Thinking deeply about various political issues

My prayer is that this journal helps in your quest to live out Romans 12 in every area of your life, including politics.

*Do not conform to the pattern of this world,
but be transformed by the renewing of your mind. Then you
will be able to test and approve what God's will is—
his good, pleasing and perfect will.*

*For by the grace given me I say to every one of you:
Do not think of yourself more highly than you ought, but
rather think of yourself with sober judgment, in accordance
with the faith God has distributed to each of you. For just
as each of us has one body with many members, and these
members do not all have the same function, so in Christ we,
though many, form one body, and each member belongs to
all the others. We have different gifts, according to the grace
given to each of us. If your gift is prophesying, then prophesy
in accordance with your faith; if it is serving, then serve;
if it is teaching, then teach; if it is to encourage, then give
encouragement; if it is giving, then give generously; if it is to
lead, do it diligently; if it is to show mercy,
do it cheerfully.*

*Love must be sincere. Hate what is evil;
cling to what is good. Be devoted to one another in love.
Honor one another above yourselves.*

Never be lacking in zeal, but keep your spiritual fervor, serving the Lord. Be joyful in hope, patient in affliction, faithful in prayer. Share with the Lord's people who are in need. Practice hospitality.

Bless those who persecute you; bless and do not curse. Rejoice with those who rejoice; mourn with those who mourn. Live in harmony with one another. Do not be proud, but be willing to associate with people of low position. Do not be conceited.

Do not repay anyone evil for evil. Be careful to do what is right in the eyes of everyone. If it is possible, as far as it depends on you, live at peace with everyone. Do not take revenge, my dear friends, but leave room for God's wrath, for it is written: "It is mine to avenge; I will repay," says the Lord. On the contrary:

"If your enemy is hungry, feed him; if he is thirsty, give him something to drink.

In doing this, you will heap burning coals on his head."

Do not be overcome by evil, but overcome evil with good.

RENEWING OF OUR MINDS

VERSE OF THE DAY

Do not conform to the pattern of this world, but be transformed
by the renewing of your mind. Then you will be able to test and approve what
God's will is—his good, pleasing and perfect will.

ROMANS 12:1-2

PRAYER

Lord, help me to see my blind spots. Renew my mind. What are the
issues, politically, where I have been conformed to the patterns of this
world? What are the issues where I have conformed to the will of a
political party, and surrendered my ability to test and approve what
your will is on that issue? I deeply desire to know your good, pleasing,
and perfect will. Help me Lord. I long to see the world through your
eyes and not my own.

REFLECTION

HONOR ONE ANOTHER ABOVE YOURSELVES

VERSE OF THE DAY

Love must be sincere. Hate what is evil;

cling to what is good. Be devoted to one another in love.

Honor one another above yourselves.

ROMANS 12:9-10

PRAYER

Lord, help my love to be sincere. Help me to love every human life that you have created. Search my heart. Show me where I have honored myself above others. Convict me, Lord. I want to bring your love to the world. This is my deepest desire. I reject the feeling of shame that the enemy is trying to heap on me, Lord, for every time I have fallen short of this command. I know that is not from you, Father. However, I do desperately want to grow in my capacity to love, and for my love to be sincere. Where have I allowed politics to get in the way of this? Help me grow, Lord. I wish to cling to what is good.

REFLECTION

DAY 3

JOYFUL, PATIENT, AND FAITHFUL

VERSE OF THE DAY

Be joyful in hope, patient in affliction, faithful in prayer.

Share with the Lord's people who are in need.

Practice hospitality.

ROMANS 12:12-13

PRAYER

Lord, thank you for being a good Father. Thank you for being the ultimate source of our hope, so that we might remain patient in affliction. Help me to always desire time with you. Imbed in me a longing to remain faithful in prayer. Search my mind and heart, Lord. What are the things in my life that have pulled me in the other direction? What idols have I created that have occasionally caused me to not want to practice hospitality and share with those in need? What has robbed me of my hope and joy? I want my joy firmly rooted in you, Father.

REFLECTION

LOVE YOUR NEIGHBOR AS YOURSELF

VERSE OF THE DAY

'Love the Lord your God with all your heart and with all your soul and with all your mind.' This is the first and greatest commandment. And the second is like it: 'Love your neighbor as yourself.'

MATTHEW 22:37-39

PRAYER

Lord, I long for this! I long for the ability to love my neighbors as myself. All of them, Father. I want to love those neighbors of mine that are hardest to love. Father, what would that even look like? How would that manifest in my life? How can I truly live this out? Lord, I can envision loving certain people this way. Help me to love every single one of your creations. I know that this is impossible on my own, but all things are possible through you. Show me the people that I currently have the hardest time loving as myself. Bring them to the top of my mind, Father. Show me what loving them would look like. Help me see any barriers that currently stand in the way. I desperately want to live out your two greatest commandments. Thank you for your patience with me on this journey.

REFLECTION

PRODUCING FRESH WATER

VERSE OF THE DAY

"With the tongue we praise our Lord and Father,
and with it we curse human beings, who have been made in God's likeness.
Out of the same mouth come praise and cursing. My brothers and sisters, this
should not be. Can both fresh water and salt water flow from the same spring?
My brothers and sisters, can a fig tree bear olives, or a grapevine bear figs?
Neither can a salt spring produce fresh water."

MATTHEW 22:37-39

PRAYER

Lord, show me the salt water in my life. Where have I allowed politics to turn my heart against your creation? Where have I used the same tongue, that I use to praise you, to curse those who were made in your likeness? Who brings out the worst in me? Forgive me, Father! I desire your heart for your creation. I desire patience and love for those I am tempted to curse. Heal my heart, Lord. Help me to turn away from this and turn back to you. Help me to accept the grace you have already given to me, through your son, for every time I have fallen short in this way. Give me a spirit of excitement to grow in this, instead of a spirit of condemnation for how I have been in the past. Thank you for your unending grace, Father.

REFLECTION

DAY 6

LET THE PEACE OF CHRIST RULE IN YOUR HEARTS

VERSE OF THE DAY

"Let the peace of Christ rule in your hearts, since as members of one body you were called to peace. And be thankful. Let the message of Christ dwell among you richly as you teach and admonish one another with all wisdom through psalms, hymns, and songs from the Spirit, singing to God with gratitude in your hearts. And whatever you do, whether in word or deed, do it all in the name of the Lord Jesus, giving thanks to God the Father through him."

COLOSSIANS 3:15-17

PRAYER

Lord, give me this heart of thankfulness. I truly desire to do everything that I do in your name, giving your thanks. I long for the peace of Christ in my heart that you have promised, if I am willing to turn my life fully over to you. Father, show me the areas of my life where I am not living this out. Whether in word or deed, where have I not fully surrendered my life to you? I want to give it all to you. I am done holding back. Whether it is my politics, my career, my relationships, my finances, or other areas of my life, I don't want to hold back any longer. Show me the parts of my life that I have been holding back. Show me my words and deeds, Father. I want to give these over to you more and more every day.

REFLECTION

SEARCH MY THOUGHTS

VERSE OF THE DAY

"Search me, God, and know my heart; test me and know my anxious thoughts. See if there is any offensive way in me, and lead me in the way everlasting."

PSALM 139:23-24

PRAYER

Yes, Lord. Yes. Show me my anxious thoughts. What is causing these? What is bringing these anxious thoughts? Show me any offensive ways in my life. What is leading me down that path? Give me the strength to cut off any voices I have allowed to gain a foothold in my life, Father, if they are pulling me away from you and your commandments. Test me. I love you so much, Lord. Thank you for your continued grace on this journey. Help me to fully accept your grace and love.

REFLECTION

DAY 8

OUT OF A PERSON'S HEART

Jesus went on: "What comes out of a person is what defiles them. For it is from within, out of a person's heart, that evil thoughts come—sexual immorality, theft, murder, adultery, greed, malice, deceit, lewdness, envy, slander, arrogance and folly. All these evils come from inside and defile a person."

MARK 7:20-23

PRAYER

Father, convict me today in the areas of my heart that still need you. Help me to approach you with humility, but not shame. I know that you are a loving Father. I know that you already know the worst inclinations of my heart. I also know that you sent your son for me, to pay a debt I could never pay, because you love me that much. Help me to accept your love today, even as you show me the evil you wish to cleanse. Show me any evil thoughts that I have allowed into my heart. What do you want to show me today, Father? What idols have I created in my life that are leading me down this path? Give me the strength to do battle against these forces that would seek to draw me away from you.

REFLECTION

DAY 9

REMOVING THE PLANK

VERSE OF THE DAY

"Do not judge, or you too will be judged. For in the same way you judge others, you will be judged, and with the measure you use, it will be measured to you. Why do you look at the speck of sawdust in your brother's eye and pay no attention to the plank in your own eye? How can you say to your brother, 'Let me take the speck out of your eye,' when all the time there is a plank in your own eye? You hypocrite, first take the plank out of your own eye, and then you will see clearly to remove the speck from your brother's eye."

MARK 7:20-23

PRAYER

Lord, what plank are you calling me to remove from my own eye? Where am I tempted to judge others before bringing my own sin before you? Help me approach others with the love and compassion that you have shown me, Father. Thank you for your forgiveness and grace. Help me to wake up each morning looking for this plank. I want to be an example of your grace and love to the world.

REFLECTION

WHERE AM I A MOCKER, LORD?

VERSE OF THE DAY

Whoever corrects a mocker invites insults; whoever rebukes
the wicked incurs abuse. Do not rebuke mockers or they will hate you; rebuke
the wise and they will love you. Instruct the wise and they will be wiser still;
teach the righteous and they will add to their learning.

PROVERBS 9:7-9

PRAYER

Lord, I truly desire to seek wisdom. I do not want to be the mocker that you warn about in Proverbs. Show me where I have refused to seek wisdom, Father. On what issues do I refuse to listen to those who might see things from an angle I have not yet considered? On what topics have I become a mocker? Remove from me the desire to always be right. Cleanse my heart of the need to stir up conflict. Place within me a heart of peace. Give me a thirst for knowledge. Guide my steps along the way, and give me the courage to break down my preconceived notions. Add to my learning, Father.

REFLECTION

FRUITS OF THE SPIRIT, PART 1

We will be spending the next three days meditating
on this passage from Galatians.

VERSE OF THE DAY

But the fruit of the Spirit is love, joy, peace, forbearance, kindness, goodness,

faithfulness, gentleness and self-control. Against such things there is no law.

Those who belong to Christ Jesus have crucified the flesh with its passions and

desires. Since we live by the Spirit, let us keep in step with the Spirit. Let us not

become conceited, provoking and envying each other.

GALATIANS 5:22-26

PRAYER

Father, I want to bear fruit. I want a life filled with love, joy, peace, and
kindness. Show me areas of my life where I can bear more fruit. Lord,
who are the people you are calling me to love more completely and
show more kindness to? What are the circumstances in my life where
I have been rejecting your offer of peace? I want more of you, Jesus. I
want more of your living through me. Give me the fruits of your Spirit.

REFLECTION

FRUITS OF THE SPIRIT, PART 2

VERSE OF THE DAY

But the fruit of the Spirit is love, joy, peace, forbearance, kindness, goodness, faithfulness, gentleness and self-control. Against such things there is no law. Those who belong to Christ Jesus have crucified the flesh with its passions and desires. Since we live by the Spirit, let us keep in step with the Spirit. Let us not become conceited, provoking and envying each other.

GALATIANS 5:22-26

PRAYER

Father, help me increase in my capacity for faithfulness, gentleness, and self-control. There are so many circumstances, Lord, that stretch me in these areas, but I know all things are possible through you. I want to be a shining example of your love to others, Father. Where are you calling me to grow in my faithfulness, gentleness, and self-control? Where have I been lacking in these fruits of the Spirit, Lord? Help me to accept your grace with these shortcomings. Give me the strength to turn back to you with these areas of my life that I have been wanting to keep for myself.

REFLECTION

FRUITS OF THE SPIRIT, PART 3

VERSE OF THE DAY

But the fruit of the Spirit is love, joy, peace, forbearance, kindness, goodness, faithfulness, gentleness and self-control. Against such things there is no law. Those who belong to Christ Jesus have crucified the flesh with its passions and desires. Since we live by the Spirit, let us keep in step with the Spirit. Let us not become conceited, provoking and envying each other.

GALATIANS 5:22-26

PRAYER

Father, I desperately desire to not become conceited. I don't want to live life provoking and envying other people. Give me your eyes to see, Lord. Search my heart and show me the ways I have fallen into the fruits of the flesh, instead of the fruits of the Spirit. What influences have I allowed to pull me down that path? What voices are you calling me to stop listening to? What activities are you calling me to stop engaging in? I want to belong fully to you, Father. I want to crucify my flesh with my passions and desires like you spoke of. I want to bear fruit. Help me, Father!

REFLECTION

THE SIN LIVING IN ME

VERSE OF THE DAY

*"For I do not do the good I want to do, but the evil I do not want
to do—this I keep on doing. Now if I do what I do not want to do, it is no
longer I who do it, but it is sin living in me that does it."*

ROMANS 7:19-20

PRAYER

Lord, forgive me! I am Paul. I feel this verse deeply, Father. I so badly
want to do good and so desperately desire to turn away from those
stumbling blocks in my life that continue to trip me up. Thank you for
your infinite grace, Lord. Thank you for being a loving Father. Thank
you for sending your son to the cross for me, knowing that I could
never fully conquer the sin in my life. Lord, let me never take that
for granted. Never let me stop appreciating your undeserved kindness
and grace. Help me, Father. What evil in my life are you calling me
to repent of? What thoughts, actions, and habits have I allowed a
foothold in my life? Convict me, Lord. Give me the strength to do
battle. I cannot do this without you.

REFLECTION

_____
_____
_____
_____
_____
_____
_____
_____
_____
_____
_____
_____
_____
_____
_____
_____
_____
_____
_____
_____
_____
_____
_____
_____
_____
_____

GUARDING OUR HEARTS

VERSE OF THE DAY

Above all else, guard your heart,

for everything you do flows from it.

PROVERBS 4:23

PRAYER

Father, show me where I am falling short in guarding my heart. What have I allowed to shape my mindset towards this world? What public figures, media personalities, social media platforms, or other items have been causing me to stray away from loving other people as myself? Jesus, you told your followers to gouge out an eye if it caused them to sin. What are you calling me to gouge out of my life, Lord? Are there channels I need to stop watching, voices I need to stop consuming, or social media platforms I need to remove from my life? I want to guard my heart, Father. Help me!

REFLECTION

HAVING THE SAME LOVE

VERSE OF THE DAY

Therefore if you have any encouragement from being united with Christ, if any comfort from his love, if any common sharing in the Spirit, if any tenderness and compassion, then make my joy complete by being like-minded, having the same love, being one in spirit and of one mind. Do nothing out of selfish ambition or vain conceit. Rather, in humility value others above yourselves, not looking to your own interests but each of you to the interests of the others.

PHILIPPIANS 2:1-4

PRAYER

Yes, Father. You have given me so much encouragement, comfort, and compassion through your son. Help me to be like-minded, Lord. Help me to take this love and compassion and share it with the world. Who are you calling me to love in this season of life, Father? Where have I been allowing selfish ambition or vain conceit to get in the way? Cleanse me of these, Lord. I want less of me and more of you. Help me to overflow with your encouragement, comfort, and joy today.

REFLECTION

IN EVERY SITUATION

VERSE OF THE DAY

Rejoice in the Lord always. I will say it again: Rejoice! Let your gentleness be evident to all. The Lord is near. Do not be anxious about anything, but in every situation, by prayer and petition, with thanksgiving, present your requests to God. And the peace of God, which transcends all understanding, will guard your hearts and your minds in Christ Jesus.

PHILIPPIANS 4:4-7

PRAYER

Father, what are you calling me to lift up to you today? What are the situations in my life that I have been anxious about and not willing to bring to you in prayer. Reveal them to me, Lord. Help me to have a heart full of thanksgiving when bringing you these requests, Father. I thirst for your peace that transcends all understanding. I want you standing guard over my heart.

REFLECTION

THINK ABOUT SUCH THINGS

VERSE OF THE DAY

Finally, brothers and sisters, whatever is true, whatever is noble, whatever is right, whatever is pure, whatever is lovely, whatever is admirable—if anything is excellent or praiseworthy—think about such things. Whatever you have learned or received or heard from me, or seen in me—put it into practice. And the God of peace will be with you.

PHILIPPIANS 4:8-9

PRAYER

Thank you, Father, for all of the amazing blessings in my life! I can frequently forget, Lord, just how many things in my life you have blessed me with. Bring these to the top of my mind today, Father. Help me to focus my mind on these blessings, along with your will in my life. Help me to spend today thinking on things that are true, noble, right, pure, lovely, admirable, excellent, and praiseworthy. When I feel the world trying to pull me in the other direction, Father, give me the strength to turn away. I love you, Lord.

REFLECTION

NO ONE CAN SERVE TWO MASTERS

VERSE OF THE DAY

"No one can serve two masters.
Either you will hate the one and love the other,
or you will be devoted to the one and despise the other."

MATTHEW 6:24

PRAYER

Father, what have I been serving? Reveal my own heart to me, Lord. I don't want to serve two masters. I want to be fully yours. Father, are there any idols in my life you are calling me to destroy? Is there anyone or anything sitting on the throne of my life that you are meant to sit on? Give me grace, Lord. Forgive me. I repent. Please do not allow me to only pay lip service to this, Father. I need you to show me the areas of my life that are dominating my mind and keeping me from loving you and loving your creation. Help me, Father.

REFLECTION

EMBRACING CORRECTION

VERSE OF THE DAY

Whoever heeds discipline shows the way to life,
but whoever ignores correction leads others astray.

PROVERBS 10:17

PRAYER

Father, when it comes to politics, where have I refused to embrace any form of correction? Show me the areas where I have been unwilling to consider any arguments, facts, or research that are not in line with my current worldview? Where have I potentially been leading others astray, Lord, due to my unwillingness to seek wisdom? Father, I want to grow. I want to seek wisdom. I want every area of my life, including my politics, to be grounded in your love and your commands. Help me to keep your love for all mankind at the center of how I approach each topic, Lord. Give me an unquenchable thirst for wisdom.

REFLECTION

WHATEVER YOU DID FOR THE LEAST OF THESE BROTHERS AND SISTERS

VERSE OF THE DAY

"Then the righteous will answer him, 'Lord, when did we see you hungry and feed you, or thirsty and give you something to drink? When did we see you a stranger and invite you in, or needing clothes and clothe you? When did we see you sick or in prison and go to visit you?'

"The King will reply, 'Truly I tell you, whatever you did for one of the least of these brothers and sisters of mine, you did for me.'

MATTHEW 25:37-40

PRAYER

Speak to me, Father. Who are you calling me to serve? I want a heart for the poor and marginalized in our society. Break my heart for what breaks yours. Where have I been turning away recently, Lord? Where have I hardened my heart? Soften it, Father. Soften my heart. Help me to see the inherent value in every single human life, even those I am most prone to turn my back on. Help me to serve you through caring for others.

REFLECTION

REMOVING THE THORNS IN MY LIFE

VERSE OF THE DAY

The seed falling among the thorns refers to someone who hears the word, but the worries of this life and the deceitfulness of wealth choke the word, making it unfruitful. But the seed falling on good soil refers to someone who hears the word and understands it. This is the one who produces a crop, yielding a hundred, sixty or thirty times what was sown.

MATTHEW 13:22-23

PRAYER

Show me my thorns, Father. What are the worries of life that have choked out your word? I want to produce a crop. I want my life to yield a hundred times what is sown. I can only do that through you, Jesus. Holy Spirit, I need you living in me. Please help me to see my own blind spots. Uncover my thorns. I am not willing to live a life that doesn't bear fruit. I refuse to allow my money, my career, or my politics to choke out your word, Father. Give me the strength to do battle against these desires.

REFLECTION

DESTROY MY WALLS

VERSE OF THE DAY

For he himself is our peace, who has made the two groups one and has destroyed the barrier, the dividing wall of hostility, by setting aside in his flesh the law with its commands and regulations. His purpose was to create in himself one new humanity out of the two, thus making peace, and in one body to reconcile both of them to God through the cross, by which he put to death their hostility. He came and preached peace to you who were far away and peace to those who were near. For through him we both have access to the Father by one Spirit.

Consequently, you are no longer foreigners and strangers, but fellow citizens with God's people and also members of his household, built on the foundation of the apostles and prophets, with Christ Jesus himself as the chief cornerstone. In him the whole building is joined together and rises to become a holy temple in the Lord. And in him you too are being built together to become a dwelling in which God lives by his Spirit.

EPHESIANS 2:14-22

PRAYER

Father, where have I kept up any dividing walls of hostility? What group of people have I hardened my heart against? Show me my thoughts, Lord. I desperately need you to heal my heart. I want your peace! I want to view every human being as fellow citizens of your Kingdom, Father. What group of people is currently a stumbling block for me? I want to love every one of your creations, Lord, regardless of their political party, race, religion, profession, country of origin, income level, or anything else. Show me my heart, Lord. Cleanse me of this desire to sort people, Father. Help me to see them through your eyes.

REFLECTION

DESIRING HUMILITY

VERSE OF THE DAY

Before destruction a man's heart is haughty,
but humility comes before honor.

PROVERBS 18:12

PRAYER

Father, I desire humility. In what areas of my life do I still lack this humility you reference frequently throughout your word? I want this in every area of my life. In what areas have I become proud? Where have I allowed my heart to become haughty and no longer seeking wisdom? Open my eyes, Father. Help me to boast only in you.

REFLECTION

NEITHER DO I CONDEMN YOU

VERSE OF THE DAY

They made her stand before the group and said to Jesus, "Teacher, this woman was caught in the act of adultery. In the Law Moses commanded us to stone such women. Now what do you say?" They were using this question as a trap, in order to have a basis for accusing him.

But Jesus bent down and started to write on the ground with his finger. When they kept on questioning him, he straightened up and said to them, "Let any one of you who is without sin be the first to throw a stone at her." Again he stooped down and wrote on the ground.

At this, those who heard began to go away one at a time, the older ones first, until only Jesus was left, with the woman still standing there. Jesus straightened up and asked her, "Woman, where are they? Has no one condemned you?"

"No one, sir," she said.

"Then neither do I condemn you," Jesus declared. "Go now and leave your life of sin."

JOHN 8:1-11

PRAYER

Forgive me, Father! Forgive me for all of the unrepented sin in my own life. Forgive me for my desire to see justice given out to others while desiring mercy for myself. Forgive me for every time I wanted to pick up a stone. Lord, what sins in my own life are you calling me to turn over to you? What are the sins in other people's lives that I fixate on, instead of approaching them with love and grace? Who are you calling me to minister to? What group of people are you telling me to no longer condemn? How can I bring your love to these people, Lord, so that they can come to know you? Father, give me the strength to accept your forgiveness and turn away from the sin in my life. Give me strength to show others the mercy you have shown me. Thank you, Father.

REFLECTION

DAY 26

UNCOVER MY EARS

VERSE OF THE DAY

"'And the word of the Lord came again to Zechariah: "This is what the Lord Almighty said: 'Administer true justice; show mercy and compassion to one another. Do not oppress the widow or the fatherless, the foreigner or the poor. Do not plot evil against each other.'"

"But they refused to pay attention; stubbornly they turned their backs and covered their ears. They made their hearts as hard as flint and would not listen to the law or to the words that the Lord Almighty had sent by his Spirit through the earlier prophets. So the Lord Almighty was very angry."

MATTHEW 13:22-23

PRAYER

Father, show me how I am like the Israelites. Show me where I have turned my back and covered my ears when it comes to your commands to show mercy and compassion. Where have I ignored your commands when it comes to fighting against oppression of the widow, the fatherless, the foreigner, or the poor? Where have I made my heart hard as flint? Forgive me, Father. Holy Spirit, invade my life! Live through me. I want to live my life according to your mission, Lord, and not my own. Thank you for your word. Thank you for your unfailing grace.

REFLECTION

BEARING FRUIT THAT WILL LAST

VERSE OF THE DAY

"As the Father has loved me, so have I loved you. Now remain in my love. If you keep my commands, you will remain in my love, just as I have kept my Father's commands and remain in his love. I have told you this so that my joy may be in you and that your joy may be complete. My command is this: Love each other as I have loved you. Greater love has no one than this: to lay down one's life for one's friends. You are my friends if you do what I command. I no longer call you servants, because a servant does not know his master's business. Instead, I have called you friends, for everything that I learned from my Father I have made known to you. You did not choose me, but I chose you and appointed you so that you might go and bear fruit—fruit that will last—and so that whatever you ask in my name the Father will give you. This is my command: Love each other.

JOHN 15:9-17

PRAYER

Father, as you have loved me, help me love others. You have appointed me to bear fruit that will last. You have commanded us to love each other. I want to honor your commands, Lord. I want you as my Lord and savior, not just savior. Rule my life, Father. What is getting in my way of loving others well? What is keeping me from having the over-the-top love for your creation that I desire? Show me the things in my life that keep getting in the way. Give me the strength to prune back any branches in my life that need pruning, so that I can be healthy and bear fruit. I want to remain in your love, Jesus.

REFLECTION

DAY 28

HOW MUCH MORE VALUABLE IS A PERSON?

VERSE OF THE DAY

*"Going on from that place, he went into their synagogue,
and a man with a shriveled hand was there. Looking for a reason to bring
charges against Jesus, they asked him, 'Is it lawful to heal on the Sabbath?'*

*He said to them, 'If any of you has a sheep and it falls into a pit on the Sabbath,
will you not take hold of it and lift it out? How much more valuable is a person than
a sheep! Therefore it is lawful to do good on the Sabbath.'*

*Then he said to the man, 'Stretch out your hand.' So he stretched it out and it
was completely restored, just as sound as the other. But the Pharisees went out
and plotted how they might kill Jesus."*

MATTHEW 12:9-13

PRAYER

Father, where have I fallen into this trap of legalism? Where have I gotten so caught up in policy debates, political philosophy, and the letter of the law that I have lost sight of the people impacted? Help me, Lord. Look into my eyes, Father, and ask me, "How much more valuable is a person?" I want to approach life with this perspective. I want to do as much good for your creation as I can. I want to lead a life of impact centered on your two greatest commandments. Help me to love others as myself today, Father.

REFLECTION

FEED MY SHEEP

When they had finished eating, Jesus said to Simon Peter,

"Simon son of John, do you love me more than these?"

"Yes, Lord," he said, "you know that I love you."

Jesus said, "Feed my lambs."

Again Jesus said, "Simon son of John, do you love me?"

He answered, "Yes, Lord, you know that I love you."

Jesus said, "Take care of my sheep."

The third time he said to him, "Simon son of John, do you love me?"

Peter was hurt because Jesus asked him the third time, "Do you love me?" He said,

"Lord, you know all things; you know that I love you."

Jesus said, "Feed my sheep."

JOHN 21:15-17

PRAYER

Father, you know I love you. You know I love you. I love you so much! I am brought to my knees by my love for you and by your love and mercy. How can I feed your sheep, Lord? How can I care for your lambs? Give me a heart of service. Break down my walls of cynicism, mistrust, and fear. Replace them with a heart of love. I want to feed your sheep. I am ready to feed your sheep. Show me how, Father. I am ready to do your will.

REFLECTION

THE GREATEST OF THESE IS LOVE

VERSE OF THE DAY

If I speak in the tongues of men or of angels, but do not have love, I am only a resounding gong or a clanging cymbal. If I have the gift of prophecy and can fathom all mysteries and all knowledge, and if I have a faith that can move mountains, but do not have love, I am nothing. If I give all I possess to the poor and give over my body to hardship that I may boast, but do not have love, I gain nothing.

Love is patient, love is kind. It does not envy, it does not boast, it is not proud. It does not dishonor others, it is not self-seeking, it is not easily angered, it keeps no record of wrongs. Love does not delight in evil but rejoices with the truth. It always protects, always trusts, always hopes, always perseveres.

Love never fails. But where there are prophecies, they will cease; where there are tongues, they will be stilled; where there is knowledge, it will pass away. For we know in part and we prophesy in part, but when completeness comes, what is in part disappears. When I was a child, I talked like a child, I thought like a child, I reasoned like a child. When I became a man, I put the ways of childhood behind me. For now we see only a reflection as in a mirror; then we shall see face to face. Now I know in part; then I shall know fully, even as I am fully known.

And now these three remain: faith, hope and love. But the greatest of these is love.

JOHN 21:15-17

PRAYER

Father, I want the love for all of mankind that you described here. I want to be filled with a love that is patient, kind, and rejoices in truth. I want to be overflowing with a love that always protects, always trusts, always hopes, and always perseveres. I am ready to embrace your love. I am ready to step away from dishonoring others, being self-seeking, keeping records of every wrong ever done against me, and being easily angered. I am ready to conquer these with love, Father. Holy Spirit, take my life. Jesus, you promised to send your Spirit to live in us. I am ready to take you up on your promise. I am ready to live a life of love. I am ready to live out your greatest two commandments, Father. I am ready to lead a life centered on loving you and loving your creation. Thank you, Father. Thank you for your continued grace, forgiveness, and love. Thank you that my hope can be in you.

REFLECTION

_____

_____

_____

_____

_____

_____

_____

_____

_____

_____

THE SEARCH FOR
WISDOM

*Instruct the wise and they will
be wiser still; teach the righteous and they
will add to their learning.*

PROVERBS 9:9

SEARCHING FOR WISDOM IN OUR
OWN POLITICAL BELIEFS

This section of the journal is designed as a place for you to work through the exercise I described in Chapter 5. There is power in stepping back from the stances we have always held and asking, "Why?"

"Do I really believe that?"

"Have I thought about this issue deeply or purely at the surface level?"

"Have I considered all sides of this topic or have I stayed within my own echo chamber, primarily consuming content that conforms to my existing world view on this issue?"

"Am I embracing the nuance and complexity of this issue?"

"How would I address this issue if I was actually in charge?"

The questions I pose in this section do not necessarily reflect my own personal views. In fact, some of them are pretty far from them! Some questions may seem extreme. That is the purpose. Most issues in politics are not as black and white as we want them to be.

This journal is for you. There is no need to win a debate. There is no reason to defend previously held positions. You don't have to go out in search of information that will make you feel more comfortable staying exactly where you are.

This portion is about seeking wisdom.

On many topics, you will come away from this exercise even more firmly rooted in your previously held position, but with more in depth reasoning behind your stance. That is fantastic. It is good to know why we believe what we believe.

On some, you may find your position changing completely. Don't fear this. The Bible tells us that it is wise to accept correction.

On some, your view may become complicated. That is not a bad thing. Some issues are so complex that we end up with extremely nuanced opinions and don't even feel completely convicted in those.

You are not supposed to solve all of the world's problems in this portion of the journal. It is simply a safe space for you to turn to the Father and ask, "Why do I believe what I believe? Are any of these beliefs becoming an idol in my life? Are there political beliefs that carry more weight in my life than they should? Do any of these beliefs go against your will in this world?

Again, this is just for you. Let's dive in.

GUN CONTROL

QUESTIONS TO CONTEMPLATE

Do I believe that the second Amendment is still necessary or should guns be outlawed entirely?

If I believe the second Amendment is still necessary, to what extent do I believe that military-grade weapons fall under this protection?

Where is the line in my mind? Only handguns? Semiautomatic? Fully automatic? Assault rifles? Sniper rifles? .50 caliber Browning machine guns? Drones capable of launching missle strikes? Tactical nuclear weapons? Biological weapons?

Why did I draw the line there?

Should there be mandatory training and special permits required for every gun? Specific types of guns?

How do I feel about universal background checks before purchasing a gun?

Should there be a wait period when buying any gun to avoid any people that are buying a weapon with ill intent?

Do I believe that there are people who should not be able to buy a gun? People on the terrorist watch list? Felons? Violent misdemeanors? Domestic abusers? Specific mental health conditions?

If I believe some of these people should not be able to buy a weapon, is that permanent? Can they after some waiting period or passing some test?

Who should be in charge of setting the line on these items and enforcing the laws surrounding gun ownership? The federal government? State government? Local governments?

Is it necessary to have a federal policy that is universal to avoid guns that are illegal in some states but not in others, traveling across state lines?

Are there any potential unintended consequences of my beliefs that I have not given consideration to?

REFLECTION

_____

_____

_____

_____

_____

_____

_____

_____

REFLECTION

REFLECTION

HEALTHCARE

QUESTIONS TO CONTEMPLATE

Do I believe that the government has an obligation to ensure affordable healthcare is available to all citizens? Why do I believe that?

If I do believe that, do I believe a single-payer system is the best solution? Or do I believe some combination of a private system with government subsidies, similar to Obamacare, is the better approach? Why do I believe that?

If I believe in an Obamacare model, what improvements would I like to see made? Why do I believe those would make the system better? Do I have evidence to support this or is it a philosophical opinion?

If I believe in a single-payer option, like Medicare for all, why is that my preference?

If one of the primary arguments for a single-payer system is the ability to negotiate from a place of strength to drive down costs, could this also be accomplished through other legislation?

Could it work to benchmark insurance payouts for various medications and procedures based on the averages of ten to fifteen nations that currently have single-payer systems? Would this be necessary to drive down cost in either case? Why or why not?

How do we ensure that we do not create an incentive structure that causes less brilliant people to want to go into healthcare?

If another argument is insurance company greed (executive compensation, corporate profit, etc.) are there other ways to attack these challenges? Why or why not?

Do I see any aspects of the United States, as a whole, that would make a single-payer system more challenging than smaller countries that have implemented it? How could we combat these challenges?

If I believe that the government does have a fundamental responsibility to ensure healthcare is affordable to everyone, but am not in favor of a single-payer system or something modeled after Obamacare, what would I like it to look like?

What gives me confidence that would work better than the other options? Is this based on facts and research, or is that simply my opinion?

If I believe that the government does not have the obligation to ensure affordable healthcare is accessible, how should we handle people without insurance?

When people don't have insurance and end up in large amounts of medical debt, a large number end up declaring bankruptcy. These bankruptcies act to drive up the cost for everyone else, so how should we approach this?

If we believe it is not our responsibility to contribute to someone else's healthcare, should hospitals refuse to serve people unless they pay up front?

What about serious situations where it is life-threatening?
Should medical bankruptcies be done away with and someone simply has to work off that debt, in some cases, for the rest of their lives?

Should we stop providing service once someone has reached a certain level of debt that they will almost certainly never be able to pay off?

How should we handle pre-existing conditions? What if a child is born with a heart defect, cancer, or some other serious condition? In a free-market system, insuring these people would never make sense without sky-high premiums. Does the government step in then to contribute? Why then?

Are there other ideas I would like to see our politicians explore that could help the overall healthcare system?

How can we prioritize wellness and overall health in advance as a country, instead of focusing all of our time on how to pay for it when we get sick?

How could these types of ideas be best implemented?
Are there any potential unintended consequences of my beliefs that I have not given consideration to?

REFLECTION

REFLECTION

REFLECTION

IMMIGRATION

QUESTIONS TO CONTEMPLATE

What level of immigration do I believe we should allow into our country each year? Do I believe in completely open borders? Completely closed borders? A specific number of new immigrants we allow in each year?

Should immigration be completely merit based and prioritize specific professions that we view as inherently more valuable to society?

Should immigration be completely compassion driven and prioritize people fleeing war-torn countries, violence, famine, etc.?

Should it be completely random and operate on more of a lottery system?

Should it have aspects of each of the scenarios described above?

How did I arrive at that conclusion?

Are there specific people I believe should be kept out? Why do I believe that?

For people that are already here, do I support a path to citizenship? Should this apply to all people or people that have been here a certain length of time? What length of time? How did I arrive at that conclusion?

If I don't believe in a path to citizenship in general, does that also apply to people currently known as Dreamers that were born here to parents that were not United States citizens but are now adults? Do I believe that we should deport these adults as well, even if they have never known any other country as their home? Why do I believe what I believe on this topic?

Do I believe that family members of existing citizens should get priority over other applicants in the immigration process?

For people that are here currently, and did not go through the legal channels to come here, do I believe that they should all be deported?

Do I believe that they should all be allowed to stay? Do I believe that there is a length of time they have been here or other criteria that would determine whether or not they could stay? Why do I believe this?

How would I approach border security if I was in charge? Why do I feel that this is the best approach? Do I feel that this strikes the right balance between prioritizing security and leading with compassion and mercy?

Are there any potential unintended consequences of my beliefs that I have not given consideration to?

REFLECTION

REFLECTION

LEGALIZATION OF MARIJUANA

QUESTIONS TO CONTEMPLATE

Do I believe that marijuana should be legalized nationwide? Would I prefer to see this decided on a state-by-state basis? Would I want to see if made illegal at the federal level, taking away states' rights to override this decision locally?

What is my opinion primarily based on? Do the facts and research back up the basis for this opinion?

If I believe marijuana should be legalized, does that apply to all drugs or is there a specific line that I would draw?

For any drugs that I would prefer to see legalized, should there be an age limit? If yes, what should that age restriction be? Does my opinion on that also apply to tobacco products and alcohol?

If I am in favor of legalization of marijuana or any other drugs, are there potential negative side effects with overuse? Have I thoroughly researched this or is this opinion?

How should we counter any potential negative side effects that come with any drug use, including substances that are already legal, like alcohol and tobacco?

How should these ideas, if any, be executed? Should it be a federal mandate, implemented locally, similar to programs like Medicaid? Should it be left to the states to come up with how to execute these programs? Should these be run federally?

If I do not believe that marijuana should be illegal, do I also believe that we should outlaw the use of other substances like alcohol and tobacco? How would I propose implementing this policy? What challenges might exist?

If I believe marijuana should remain illegal, but alcohol and tobacco should remain legal, how did I arrive at that conclusion? Was this a public health decision? Was it about protecting an individual from themselves?

Have I thoroughly researched the impacts on the human brain that occur under the influence of alcohol, tobacco, and marijuana?

Have I thoroughly researched the health implications of consuming alcohol, tobacco, and marijuana over time?

Are there any potential unintended consequences of my beliefs that I have not given consideration to?

REFLECTION

REFLECTION

PROTECTING THE ENVIRONMENT

QUESTIONS TO CONTEMPLATE

Do I believe that global warming is occurring and that the human race is contributing to it? Have I thoroughly studied this topic from both sides?

Have I stepped outside my own political party and looked at expert opinions from the other side and from other countries as well?

Do I believe that we should prioritize keeping lakes and rivers free of chemical pollutants? Why or why not?

Do I believe that we should prioritize air quality? Why or why not?

Do I believe that we should allow offshore drilling in protected natural wildlife preserves? Why or why not?

Do I believe we should continue to build new power plants that utilize nonrenewable resources? Why or why not?

Should we regulate the use of chemicals in agriculture that have been proven to cause negative health effects? Why or why not?

If I would advocate that the government should not be heavily involved in environmental issues, would I feel the same way if the new power plant was being put in one hundred yards from my house?

If I owned property on the body of water that was having chemicals dumped in? If the drilling was going to be happening at my favorite vacation destination? Would I feel differently if I felt the impact more directly?

If I would advocate for more strict government regulation, how should we go about a smooth transition of the existing fossil fuel workforce? What programs should we be exploring to retrain these workers to step into a new job at a comparable wage?

If the new jobs were not going to be able to offer a comparable wage, do I believe the government should step in and supplement their income for the greater good of the environment?

Would I feel this same way about other industries that are going to be impacted by factors outside of their control in the coming decades?

Who gets to decide this and where would we draw the line?

How should we work with the rest of the world to address this issue?

How should we balance the responsibility of developed nations and developing nations?

If I believe that the government should step in, what programs would move the needle the most?

Do I support a form of cap and trade?

Do I support subsidies for individual consumers who want to install renewable energy systems at their own homes or convert to energy efficient appliances, light bulbs, etc.?

If I do believe in this, to what extent should these be subsidized?

Would these same subsidies apply to businesses, schools, hospitals, etc.? To the same levels? To a higher level or lower level? Why?

Should we subsidize utility companies to aggressively change over to renewable energy?

Should these subsidies be given as the old infrastructure phases out or as there is need for more capacity?

Should subsidies be so great that there would actually be incentive to convert to renewable sources ahead of any scheduled infrastructure projects?

How should we pay for these programs?

Should this money come from cuts in spending elsewhere? Where should we cut?

Should this money come from increased taxes of some sort? What specific tax increases would I advocate for?

Should we simply print money and deal with the potential inflation that could accompany this?

Are there any potential unintended consequences of my beliefs that I have not given consideration to?

REFLECTION

REFLECTION

REFLECTION

TAX POLICY

QUESTIONS TO CONTEMPLATE

Do I agree with our current structure of progressive tax brackets, where the percent of income a person pays increases as their level of income increases?

If not, what type of tax structure would I advocate for?

Should we have lower income taxes, but a higher sales tax? If yes, should the same tax rate apply to all items, or should this be based on the type of good purchased?

Should luxury items be taxed at a higher percentage and basic necessities taxed at a lower rate or not at all? Who would decide how these were determined?

If I was in charge of setting the individual tax rates for various income levels, where would I set the rates? How did I decide on that?

If I was in charge of setting the tax rates for business profits, where would I set the rates? Would this be a flat rate or should we adopt a progressive structure for businesses as well?

Should this be different for LLCs, S-Corps, and C-Corps? Should it be different for publicly versus privately held companies?

What would I allow to be written off as business expenses? How would I go about closing tax loopholes for corporations? Would I want these closed at all?

If I was in charge of setting the tax rates for capital gains, where would I set the rates? Would this be a flat rate or should we adopt a progressive structure for businesses as well? Should this be a different structure for different types of capital gains?

How do we make sure that we have a tax code that doesn't cause businesses to simply move operations overseas? Have I put time into looking at tax rates on business profits in other countries to see how the United States actually compares?

Are there other ways to incentivize businesses to stay in the United States and keep jobs here as well?

Do I believe that there should be an inheritance tax? Should this only exist above a certain amount? What would that amount be? Should this be a progressive tax structure as well or a flat percentage?

Should we have a wealth tax once a person reaches a certain level of net worth? Above what level? What would all be included? How would this be implemented?

Should we have a larger standard deduction that individuals and families can take, removing the need to itemize; or should we have a lower standard deduction and incentivize itemized deductions? Why?

What items should people still be able to deduct if they take the standard deduction? Any at all? Education? Childcare? What else?

What do I think about the current tax credits for each child? Should there be none at all? A lower amount? Higher amount?

What issues are we attempting to solve through these tax credits? Are there other ways that may accomplish this more effectively and drive better results for those families?

Should we use tax credits more aggressively to incentivize behavior in businesses? What would I like to see incentivized?

When I think about tax policy, have I done research on what is done in different countries and the impact of these policies?

Are my opinions rooted in facts or philosophy?

Are there any potential unintended consequences of my beliefs that I have not given consideration to?

REFLECTION

REFLECTION

REFLECTION

MILITARY INTERVENTION

QUESTIONS TO CONTEMPLATE

Do I believe that the United States should ever use the military to intervene in conflicts that do not directly threaten the security of our country?

How should we think about individual conflicts?

When a dictator is committing mass-atrocities on their own civilians, should we step in? If yes, how bad would these have to become to warrant the United States getting involved?

Should we get involved when there is mass-imprisonment based on race, religion, or other factors? What would constitute mass? What about displacing people from their homes for the same reasons? What about genocide? How many deaths would constitute genocide in my eyes?

When it is a direct threat to our national security, what level of urgency and severity of threat would constitute use of the military?

Does this include threats to our economic security? Disruption of shipping lanes? Disruption of oil production? Other economic impacts?

What options should we explore first before ever considering military intervention? Direct diplomacy? Diplomatic efforts that loop in multiple allies? Work through the UN?

Should we first use sanctions wherever possible? What form should these sanctions take?

Should we work to ensure the general population is impacted as little as possible by any economic sanctions and target these at senior leadership? How can we do this in a way that trickles down to the people as little as possible?

If the goal of sanctions is to create enough social unrest that the people of the country turn against the government, what should our involvement be if this occurs?

If diplomatic efforts and sanctions are not having the desired impact, should the United States be willing to intervene with the use of military force without the support of our allies?

When is it okay to use drone strikes on suspected terrorists? How much risk of civilian casualties should we be willing to accept?

How certain of an imminent threat should we be before utilizing drone strikes? How serious of a threat does this need to be?

Have I spent time researching the impacts of the United States drone programs under Bush, Obama, and Trump to form these opinions?

Do I believe the theory that the use of drone strikes can be counterproductive for countering terrorism because the loss of civilian life ends up being a powerful recruiting tool for terrorist groups? Why or why not?

If I was the president and the weight of these decisions fell on my shoulders, would I feel differently about any of the answers to the questions above?

Are there any potential unintended consequences of my beliefs that I have not given consideration to?

REFLECTION

_____

_____

_____

_____

_____

_____

_____

_____

_____

_____

_____

_____

_____

_____

_____

_____

REFLECTION

REFLECTION

REFLECTION

ADDITIONAL TOPICS

The topics addressed in this journal are just the start. This is not meant to be comprehensive. In the following pages, I would encourage you to take this exercise and continue it on your own. What topics would you like to dive into further? What are topics that naturally get you fired up and ready to debate? What topics always seem to grab your attention? What are topics you are prone to naturally dismiss the other side as "too radically conservative" or "too radically liberal" and never fully engage at a substantive level?

Continue to do this hard work of diving deep into your own beliefs on a variety of political issues!

Lean into the discomfort.

Embrace the nuance.

Accept that issues are frequently far more complicated than we might want to admit.

Seek wisdom.

Remember to keep the love of God and the love of others at the center of it all.

It truly is worth the effort.

REFLECTION

REFLECTION

REFLECTION

REFLECTION

THE POWER OF YOUR REVIEW

If "The Politically Homeless Christian" spoke to you and was a source of encouragement for you in your walk with God, I would sincerely appreciate it if you would consider writing a review of the book on Amazon. This is extremely encouraging for me, but also very helpful for other potential readers as well!

THE POLITICALLY HOMELESS CHRISTIAN JOURNAL

If you would like additional copies of the journal portion
of this book, they can be ordered separately through Amazon.

We would also like to make this journal as readily accessible to
anyone who would like one, so you can also get a free digital copy at:

WWW.THEPOLITICALLYHOMELESSCHRISTIAN.COM/JOURNAL

I hope that you found it helpful and that it continues to draw you
closer to the Father as we seek to conquer political idolatry, reject
polarization, and recommit to God's greatest two commandments!

Thank you for reading.

God Bless,

Aaron

ABOUT THE AUTHOR

Aaron Schafer is a Christian author, blogger, podcaster, and motivational speaker. Through his blog and podcast, Fertile Soil, Aaron seeks to help his readers and listeners create fertile soil in their lives for God's word to take root and produce one hundred times what was sown. Aaron previously ran the Young Adult Community at Trinity Church in Lansing, MI, and has been heavily involved in local outreach, youth ministry, and sports ministry as well. Aaron is the author of *The Politically Homeless Christian: How to Conquer Political Idolatry, Reject Polarization, and Recommit to God's Greatest Two Commandments*. In this book Aaron explores how the American Church has allowed politics to play a large role in shaping our identities and how we can break free from this cycle so that we can love God and love others better through our politics.